REBUILDING GOD'S CITY

Israel Returns from Exile

JOHN MACARTHUR

THOMAS NELSON
Since 1798

NASHVILLE   DALLAS   MEXICO CITY   RIO DE JANEIRO

Published in Nashville, Tennessee, by Thomas Nelson. Thomas Nelson is a trademark of Thomas Nelson, Inc.

Published in association with the literary agency of Wolgemuth & Associates, Inc.

Layout, design, and writing assistance by Gregory C. Benoit Publishing, Old Mystic, CT. ⅁ͳB

Thomas Nelson, Inc. titles may be purchased in bulk for educational, business, fund-raising, or sales promotional use. For information, please e-mail *SpecialMarkets@ThomasNelson.com*.

MacArthur Old Testament Study Guide Series, Volume 12

Rebuilding God's City: Israel Returns from Exile

ISBN 978-1-4185-3694-7

Printed in the United States of America

10 11 12 13 QG 5 4 3 2

CONTENTS

JERUSALEM IN NEHEMIAH'S TIME

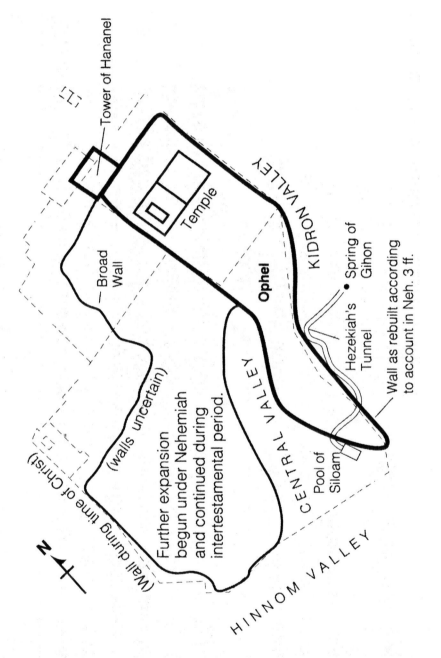

Tower of Hananel

Broad Wall

Temple

Ophel

KIDRON VALLEY

Spring of Gihon

Hezekiah's Tunnel

Wall as rebuilt according to account in Neh. 3 ff.

(walls uncertain)

Further expansion begun under Nehemiah and continued during intertestamental period.

CENTRAL VALLEY

Pool of Siloam

(Wall during time of Christ)

HINNOM VALLEY

N

INTRODUCTION

God had warned the nation of Israel that He would send them into foreign captivity if they persisted in idolatry. Yet they ignored God and ran headlong into disobedience. True to His word, God used the Babylonians and Assyrians to evict Israel from her land, destroy the city of Jerusalem, and plunder the temple. With her people in captivity, it appeared that Israel had no hope and no future.

But God had also promised that the captivity of Israel would last only seventy years, and at the end of that time He raised up Zerubbabel, Ezra, Nehemiah, and others to lead His people back to Jerusalem and begin rebuilding the city. He then sent several prophets to His people, including Haggai and Zechariah. Under this godly leadership, the people of Israel got a new start. Unfortunately—and predictably—the Israelites failed again, and went back to their idolatrous ways.

In these twelve studies, we will jump back and forth in chronological history, looking at one historical period and then skipping forward or backward in time as needed. As we examine the hard work involved in rebuilding the temple and the city walls, we will discover what it means to be a godly leader. We will also see that apart from the new covenant and the Messiah, the Israelites found it impossible to obey the Law. But through it all, we will learn some precious truths about the character of God, and we will see His great faithfulness in keeping His promises. We will learn, in short, what it means to walk by faith.

⌁ WHAT WE'LL BE STUDYING ⌁

This study guide is divided into four distinct sections in which we will examine selected Bible passages:

SECTION 1: HISTORY. In this first section, we will focus on the historical setting of our Bible text. These five lessons will give a broad overview of the people, places, and events that are important to this study. They will also provide the background for the next two sections. This is our most purely historical segment, focusing simply on what happened and why.

SECTION 2: CHARACTERS. The four lessons in this section will give us an opportunity to zoom in on the characters from our Scripture passages. Some of these people were introduced in section 1, but in this part of the study guide we will take a much closer look at these personalities. Why did God see fit to include them in His Book in the first place? What made them unique? What can we learn from their lives? In this practical section, we will answer all of these questions and more, as we learn how to live wisely by emulating the wisdom of those who came before us.

SECTION 3: THEMES. Section 3 consists of two lessons in which we will consider some of the broader themes and doctrines touched on in our selected Scripture passages. This is the guide's most abstract portion, wherein we will ponder specific doctrinal and theological questions that are important to the church today. As we ask what these truths mean to us as Christians, we will also look for practical ways to base our lives upon God's truth.

SECTION 4: SUMMARY. In our final section, we will look back at the principles that we have discovered in the scriptures throughout this study guide. These will be our "takeaway" principles, those which permeate the Bible passages that we have studied. As always, we will be looking for ways to make these truths a part of our everyday lives.

✌ ABOUT THE LESSONS ✍

❧ Each study begins with an introduction that provides the background for the selected Scripture passages.

❧ To assist you in your reading, a section of notes—a miniature Bible commentary of sorts—offers both cultural information and additional insights.

❧ A series of questions is provided to help you dig a bit deeper into the Bible text.

❧ Overriding principles brought to light by the Bible text will be studied in each lesson. These principles summarize a variety of doctrines and practical truths found throughout the Bible.

❧ Finally, additional questions will help you mine the deep riches of God's Word and, most importantly, to apply those truths to your own life.

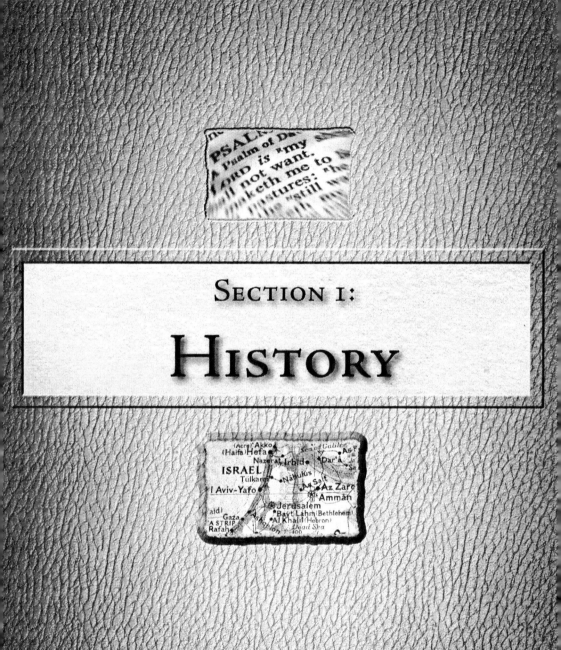

SECTION 1:

HISTORY

In This Section:

Returning from Exile

2 Chronicles 36; Ezra 1

∽ Historical Background ∽

In 605 BC, King Nebuchadnezzar of Babylon invaded Judah and began to take Jews into captivity. (The nation of Israel had been carried away by the Assyrians more than a century earlier.) About twenty years later, in 586 BC, Nebuchadnezzar destroyed the walls around Jerusalem, set fire to the Lord's temple in the heart of the city, and carried the remaining Jews into Babylonian captivity.

These events did not occur without warning. The Lord had told the Jews many centuries earlier that, if they refused to obey His Word, He would send them into exile. But despite the people's sins, when the Babylonians destroyed the temple, Jeremiah prophesied that the Jews would remain in captivity for only seventy years. Then they would begin to return to Jerusalem to rebuild God's chosen city. It is at the end of this seventy-year period that our study opens—but by this time Babylon has collapsed and been absorbed by the Persian Empire, under the reign of Cyrus. The year was 538 BC.

∽ Reading 2 Chronicles 36:11–21 ∽

The Last King of Judah: *Our studies open with a look back at the Babylonian invasion of Judah, and what led up to it.*

11. Zedekiah: Zedekiah became king in Judah around 597 BC. He was the last king of Judah, and ended a succession of wicked leaders. The nation of Israel had been divided into two kingdoms, Israel and Judah, hundreds of years earlier, and Israel had long since gone into captivity. See book 10 in this series, *Losing the Promised Land*, for more information.

12. He did evil in the sight of the Lord: Many of the kings of Judah, and most of the kings of Israel, had led God's people away from His Word into idolatry. The Lord had warned the Jews repeatedly that He would send them into captivity if they followed after false gods (Deuteronomy 28).

Jeremiah the prophet: Jeremiah wrote the book of Lamentations to mourn the destruction of the temple, which occurred when Zedekiah was king (586 BC).

13. King Nebuchadnezzar: Nebuchadnezzar was the king of Babylon at this time. Under his leadership, the empire grew to its greatest height. See book 11 in this series, *God's Presence During Hardship*, for more information on Babylon and Nebuchadnezzar.

14. all the abominations of the nations: These included idolatry, child sacrifice, sexual perversion, denial of God as the Creator, and much more. All these pagan practices are abundant in modern Western society.

defiled the house of the Lord: When God's people incorporated pagan practices into their worship, they defiled His temple. This resulted in swift judgment from God.

God's Faithfulness: *The people of Judah had been constantly unfaithful to the Lord, but He had proven completely faithful to them—even at cost to Himself.*

15. rising up early and sending them: The Lord was constantly faithful to His people, despite their unfaithfulness to Him. The figure of speech here suggests that He went out of His way to lead them back to Him, going to great lengths, and at immense cost, by sending prophets again and again to urge Israel and Judah to obey His Word.

because He had compassion on His people: Here we learn why God went to such lengths to turn His people back to Him: because He loved them! We will see more of God's compassion in these studies as we learn that His hand of discipline was tempered with grace when He gathered His people and returned them to Jerusalem. Yet His compassion is most clearly expressed in the life and person of Jesus Christ. God sent His only Son expressly to die for our sins, and there can be no greater expression of love than that.

16. mocked ... despised ... scoffed: The world has always treated the things of God with contempt, and still does so today, but this sin was committed by God's own people. It was this contempt that ultimately brought His discipline upon the nation of Judah.

17. the king of the Chaldeans: That is, Nebuchadnezzar. Chaldea was absorbed into the Babylonian Empire, yet the empire was interchangeably referred to by both names.

19. burned the house of God, broke down the wall of Jerusalem: In 597 BC, King Nebuchadnezzar carried ten thousand people into captivity from

Judah, including the prophet Ezekiel. (He had carried captives from Judah in several waves, beginning in 605 BC.) Zerubbabel and Ezra would later lead people back to Jerusalem to begin rebuilding the temple, and Nehemiah would lead the work of rebuilding the walls.

20. UNTIL THE RULE OF THE KINGDOM OF PERSIA: Cyrus conquered Babylon in 539 BC. He allowed Jews to begin returning to Jerusalem the following year.

21. UNTIL THE LAND HAD ENJOYED HER SABBATHS: The Lord had commanded His people to allow their land to lie fallow every seven years, neither planting crops nor reaping (Leviticus 25:4). Evidently, they had failed to obey that command beginning around the time when Eli was high priest (c. 1107–1067 BC). The Lord had warned the Jews that He would enforce the Sabbath rest on His promised land if they failed to keep it (Leviticus 26:27–46), and Jeremiah prophesied that the people would remain in captivity for seventy years, one year for every Sabbath they neglected (Jeremiah 25:1–11).

⤳ READING EZRA 1:1–7 ⤶

CYRUS THE GREAT: *Seventy years later, the Lord raises up a Gentile leader who will send the Jews back home: Cyrus, king of Persia.*

1. BY THE MOUTH OF JEREMIAH: See Jeremiah 25.

THE LORD STIRRED UP THE SPIRIT OF CYRUS: Throughout these studies, we will see how God used the deeds of men—both good and evil—to accomplish His sovereign purposes. Even when circumstances seemed dark and hopeless, He was still in control, and He was still working out His promises for His people.

2. THE LORD GOD OF HEAVEN HAS GIVEN ME: Cyrus evidently recognized the sovereign hand of God in his life. He acknowledged that he held power in Persia only because the Lord had given it to him—even though he probably did not worship Jehovah as the only true God. Josephus, the Jewish historian, wrote that Daniel was Cyrus's prime minister, and that he read to the king Isaiah's prophecies in which Cyrus was mentioned by name—more than a century before Cyrus was born (Isaiah 44:28). According to Josephus, this led Cyrus to make his decree allowing the Jews to return to Jerusalem.

4. LET THE MEN OF HIS PLACE HELP HIM: Cyrus commanded the neighbors of the returning Jews to assist them with finances and goods for their trip and for the work of rebuilding the temple in Jerusalem. This was reminiscent of the Israelites' preparations for the exodus from Egypt, when the Lord had them ask their neighbors for gold, silver, and clothing (Exodus 12:35–36).

5. **ALL WHOSE SPIRITS GOD HAD MOVED:** The Hebrew word here literally means "to rouse up or awaken," and is the same expression used of Cyrus in verse 1. The Lord stirred the hearts of His people, making many of them restless and unsettled in the knowledge that His temple was lying in ruins back in Judah. The Jews were not enslaved in Persia; they were permitted to live as all other Persians lived, and many had risen to prosperity and influence. It is possible, therefore, that God's people had become comfortable and complacent with their lot in Persia, so the Lord stirred their hearts to be grieved over the desecration of His holy temple and His chosen city. The important thing to note, however, is that this work of rebuilding was motivated and directed by God, not by men or by a charismatic leader. "Unless the LORD builds the house, they labor in vain who build it" (Psalm 127:1).

6. **WILLINGLY OFFERED:** Here again we are reminded of the Israelites' exodus from Egypt. But in this case there is a hint of goodwill involved, suggesting that the Jews' fellow countrymen were glad to assist them in rebuilding the Lord's house. In Egypt, the Jews had been slaves, and the Egyptians despised them, so the Jews "plundered the Egyptians" (Exodus 12:36).

⌁ FIRST IMPRESSIONS ⌁

1. *Why did God send the Jews into captivity? Why did He limit the captivity to seventy years?*

2. *How did God's people drift away from Him into idolatry? What contributed to their sin? What did God do to turn them back to Himself?*

3. In what ways did God show compassion to the Jews over the centuries? In what ways was He showing compassion even in sending them into captivity?

4. What does the Bible mean when it says the Lord "stirred up" the hearts of the Jews? Why was this needed? What was He trying to accomplish?

⤳ Some Key Principles ⤳

God keeps *all* His promises.

God had promised His people, "If you diligently obey the voice of the Lord your God, to observe carefully all His commandments which I command you today, that the Lord your God will set you high above all nations of the earth" (Deuteronomy 28:1). Under the reign of David, the nation of Israel obeyed the Lord's commands, and God kept that promise, subduing all the nation's enemies and giving Israel peace and prosperity. But God had made another promise in that same passage. "But it shall come to pass, if you do not obey the voice of the Lord your God, to observe carefully all His commandments and His statutes which I command you today, that all these curses will come upon you and overtake you: . . . You shall beget sons and daughters, but they shall not be yours; for they shall go into captivity" (vv. 15, 41). Under the reign of Solomon and beyond, the nation's kings began to lead God's people away from obedience and into idolatry, and God proved faithful to His second promise as well.

When the time came for Judah to go into captivity, the Lord promised His people that they would return to Jerusalem in seventy years—and He kept that promise too. He raised up Nebuchadnezzar to carry the nation into Babylon; then He raised up Cyrus to absorb Babylon into Persia and set His people free. He holds sovereign control over all human affairs, and He can raise up an empire or throw it down as He sees fit—but whatever happens, He always keeps His promises.

God has not changed since the time of Ezra and Nehemiah. He has given many promises to Christians, both of blessing and of discipline, and He still keeps those promises. And one of the most important promises of all is this: "For God so loved the world that He gave His only begotten Son, that whoever believes in Him should not perish but have everlasting life. For God did not send His Son into the world to condemn the world, but that the world through Him might be saved. He who believes in Him is not condemned; but he who does not believe is condemned already, because he has not believed in the name of the only begotten Son of God" (John 3:16–18). God will keep His promise of eternal life to anyone who accepts His Son, Jesus; but He will also keep His promise of eternal judgment for anyone who rejects His Son. If you do not know Jesus as your Lord and Savior, claim God's promise of salvation right now—because God keeps *all* His promises.

The Lord sends discipline to help us, not to harm us.

The Lord sent the Babylonian army into Judah to carry His people into captivity when they turned away from Him and pursued nonexistent, pagan gods. But two things are important for us to remember: first, the people had been unfaithful to God for centuries (with brief periods of revival during that time), demonstrating His great patience and grace; second, the Lord sent the Jews into captivity to discipline them and turn them back to Himself, *not* to destroy them. This was a loving but stern Father's hand of correction, not a harsh judge's verdict of condemnation.

The author of Chronicles made it clear that the Lord had patiently endured hundreds of years of disobedience in His people, "rising up early and sending" His prophets to remind them of His Word again and again, "because He had compassion on His people and on His dwelling place" (2 Chronicles 36:15). And even in the midst of discipline, the Lord demonstrated His compassion and love by raising up a new king who would send His people back to Jerusalem, and by restricting the captivity to a relatively short seventy years. Jeremiah prophesied concerning this time: "For thus says the LORD: After seventy years are completed at Babylon, I will visit you and perform My good word toward you, and cause you to return to this place. For I know the thoughts that I think toward you, says the LORD, thoughts of peace and not of evil, to give you a future and a hope" (Jeremiah 29:10–11).

The whole reason the Lord sent His people into captivity was to turn their hearts back to Him. "Then you will call upon Me and go and pray to Me," He said, "and I will listen to you. And you will seek Me and find Me, when you search for Me with all your heart" (vv. 12–13). His ways have not changed today. The Lord may send discipline into your life, but He does so in order to draw you toward Himself—not to push you away. When hardship enters your life, seek His face. He has promised that you will find Him.

This world is not our home.

The people of Judah had been carried away to captivity, but they were not made slaves as they had been many centuries earlier in Egypt. Rather, they were allowed to establish relatively normal lives within the new land, and many Jews had risen to levels of power and prosperity. Daniel, for example, had served at least three different kings as a close personal counselor. Yet this relative freedom brought a danger that the Israelites had not faced when they were slaves: the danger of complacency. Many of God's people had become quite comfortable in the Persian captivity, probably fitting in to their new society and doing well.

The problem was that God did not intend for them to make their home in Persia; their home was in Jerusalem, and He did not want them to put down roots elsewhere. God's temple was in ruins and Judah's walls lay in rubble, and the Lord grieved over that situation. He wanted His people to share those priorities and to long to return to their proper land to worship and serve God as He had ordained for them. The world in which they'd grown content was *not* their home.

This is equally true for Christians today. This world is not our home! It is not wrong to pursue a career or to establish a home, but the Lord does not want His people to lose their eternal focus. He wants them to remember that the things of eternity are what matter most, not the things of this world. Paul wrote, "Set your mind on things above, not on things on the earth. For you died, and your life is hidden with Christ in God" (Colossians 3:2–3). He was reminding us that, by being born again into the salvation of Christ, we have died to the things of this world. And if we are dead to this world, then there is no purpose in trying to make our home here. Our life is with Christ in eternity, and that is where our focus needs to remain.

⌒ Digging Deeper ⌒

5. What promises did God keep in these passages? What part did the behavior and attitudes of the Jews play in God's promises?

6. Why did God choose to use Nebuchadnezzar and Cyrus to fulfill His plans? What does this suggest about His sovereignty?

7. Why did God need to "arouse" the hearts of His people to return to Jerusalem? What worldly elements tend to lull Christians into complacency?

8. When has the Lord sent discipline into your life? What was He trying to accomplish? How did you respond?

9. Have you accepted Jesus as your Lord and Savior? If not, what is preventing you from doing so right now?

10. What might the Lord be "stirring up" your heart to do at present? What things of this world might be distracting you from sharing His priorities?

REBUILDING THE TEMPLE

⌁ HISTORICAL BACKGROUND ⌁

During the exodus from Egypt, the Lord had demonstrated His presence with His people in a variety of tangible ways. He showed that He was with them by providing a heavy cloud cover during the day to shield the people from the desert sun. By night, He provided a dramatic pillar of fire to illuminate the darkness. But beyond those manifestations, the Lord commanded the people to construct a portable temple that they were to set up whenever they made camp, and at the center of this tabernacle was the ark of the covenant.

The ark represented God's chosen place of meeting with His people, and it was a physical manifestation of His presence wherever they went. Many generations later, King Solomon built a magnificent permanent temple in Jerusalem to house the ark, and this was the Lord's chosen place for His people to assemble for corporate worship. However, when Nebuchadnezzar carried the Jews into captivity, he destroyed that temple and absconded with the ark.

In this study, the Jews have returned from exile to Jerusalem, and it is time to begin work on rebuilding the temple. They gather together as one—and then we get a surprise: they don't begin work on the temple, but instead they rebuild the altar that will go *inside* the temple. At first glance, this might seem like building one's living room furniture before building the house; but in reality, it demonstrates a correct order of priorities in God's prescribed worship. We will discover that even without the ark of the covenant, God was still with His people—because it is people who comprise God's ultimate temple, not a building of bricks and mortar.

⌁ READING EZRA 3:1–13 ⌁

BUILDING THE ALTAR: *The returning Jews gather in Jerusalem, where they will rebuild the temple—but they start by building the altar.*

1. **THE SEVENTH MONTH:** That is, September–October 537 BC. In the seventh month, the Jews celebrated three very important annual observances: the Feast of Trumpets (Numbers 29:1–6), the Day of Atonement (Numbers 29:7–11), and the Feast of Tabernacles (Numbers 29:12–38).

THE PEOPLE GATHERED TOGETHER AS ONE MAN: That is, the people who had chosen to return to Jerusalem. Their unity of purpose here demonstrated that they were deeply concerned with restoring the forms of worship that the Lord had commanded under Moses. It also suggests that the Spirit of God was at work in their hearts, stirring them up to obedience just as He had done with Cyrus and others in Ezra 1.

2. **JESHUA ... ZERUBBABEL:** Jeshua was the high priest, and Zerubbabel was the head of the tribe of Judah. It is significant that these two important men led the Jews in returning to Jerusalem. The kings and priests of Judah and Israel had previously led the people *away* from God, but now the nation's leaders, both civic and spiritual, were leading the people back to obedience to His Word.

BUILT THE ALTAR OF THE GOD OF ISRAEL: It is also significant that the very first act of rebuilding was the altar, rather than the temple or the city walls. This demonstrated that the Jews' first priority was in offering sacrifices and repenting of their sins, taking precedence over any other act of worship and even over their own physical safety. The people were trusting God to protect them while they obeyed His commands.

3. **FEAR HAD COME UPON THEM:** The "people of those countries" were settlers who had moved into Jerusalem during the seventy years that the Jews were in captivity. They saw the returning Jews as a tremendous threat to their possessions, land, and way of life; they viewed the land as their own by right of seventy years' occupation, while the Jews viewed it as theirs by virtue of God's command. We can still see this conflict occurring in the Middle East today.

LAYING THE FOUNDATION: *Having established obedience to God's Word, the people now turn their attention to the mechanics of building the temple.*

4. **THE FEAST OF TABERNACLES:** Also called the Feast of Booths, commemorating the Israelites' wandering in the wilderness during their exodus from Egypt (Leviticus 23:33–43).

5. **A FREEWILL OFFERING TO THE LORD:** In addition to reinstituting the sacrifices and feasts that God had commanded, the people also began offering voluntary tithes—all prior to rebuilding the temple. This demonstrated that worship of the Lord consists of confession and repentance of sins, worship, and giving—not meeting

inside a building. The building came later, but only after proper worship and obedience had been reestablished.

6. THE FOUNDATION OF THE TEMPLE OF THE LORD HAD NOT BEEN LAID: In a spiritual sense, the people were laying a firm foundation for the temple by obeying His Word. Obedience is more important to God's church than bricks and mortar.

7. THEY ALSO GAVE MONEY TO THE MASONS AND THE CARPENTERS: The Jews gave freely of their possessions, time, and skills to the building of the temple, but they did not ask foreigners to donate; they paid laborers and manufacturers the proper rates. This is not to say that they would not have accepted gifts if offered, but they did not expect that of foreigners, nor did they try to get things for free. As David said, "I will not take what is yours for the LORD, nor offer burnt offerings with that which costs me nothing" (1 Chronicles 21:24).

CEDAR LOGS . . . TO JOPPA: The workmen loaded cedar logs onto ships in Tyre and Sidon to the north, on the coast of the Mediterranean (or Great Sea), then sailed them south to Joppa, which was approximately forty miles from Jerusalem. (See the map in the introduction.).

8. IN THE SECOND MONTH OF THE SECOND YEAR: April–May 536 BC. This officially ended the seventy-year captivity that began in 605 BC. Once again, we see that construction of the temple did not even begin until all the elements of obedience and worship were in place.

WEEPING AND REJOICING: *The people gather in unity and respond to the preliminary construction—some with weeping, some with shouts of joy.*

ALL THOSE WHO HAD COME OUT OF THE CAPTIVITY: Once again, we see the unity and wholeheartedness of God's people, joining together as one to participate in the building of the temple, just as they had shown unity in obedience.

11. THEY SANG RESPONSIVELY: This song of praise is evidently from Psalm 136:1. The priests might have sung, "Oh, give thanks to the LORD," and then one group of the people would respond with, "For He is good!" The second group of the people would then respond, "For His mercy endures forever toward Israel."

12. OLD MEN . . . WEPT WITH A LOUD VOICE: These old men had been young when carried into captivity, and they would have remembered Solomon's temple, which stood in Jerusalem at the time. They grieved over the lost splendor of Solomon's structure, over the lost treasures that it contained—but most of all, they wept over the fact that the ark of the covenant was gone, and with it the manifestation of the Lord's presence.

YET MANY SHOUTED ALOUD FOR JOY: In spite of the loss of the ark, God was still with His people—and that alone was cause for joyful shouting and praise (Zechariah 4:9–10).

13. THE SOUND WAS HEARD AFAR OFF: The obedient praise and worship of God's people carries a profound testimony to the world around us, drawing people toward the Lord just as curiosity might have drawn neighboring people toward Jerusalem on this day.

⤳ FIRST IMPRESSIONS ⤳

1. *Why does this passage reiterate that the people gathered "as one man"? What does this indicate? What drew them together?*

2. *Why did the people build the altar before the temple that would house it? before the walls that would protect them? What does this indicate about God's priorities?*

3. Why had fear come upon the people (v. 3)? What did this have to do with rebuilding the altar?

4. What was involved in the actual building of the temple? What roles did the people play in the process? What did the construction cost them?

⌁ Some Key Principles ⌁

God dwells in believers, not in a temple.

Cyrus allowed the Jews to return to Jerusalem for the express purpose of rebuilding the Lord's temple there; yet the people did not immediately turn their attention to that construction project. The first thing they did was rebuild the altar—even though the altar would eventually be housed within the temple. Their top priority was being personally and corporately obedient to God's Word, not constructing a building in which to worship.

Their priorities demonstrated that they understood God's priorities. The people knew that "to obey is better than sacrifice, and to heed [God's Word] than the fat of rams" (1 Samuel 15:22). Yet in those days, the Lord's presence was represented by the temple, and its completion was important to the proper worship of His people. This emphasis on personal and corporate sacrifice underscored the fact that the Lord is more concerned with our obedience than with our outward shows of worship.

When Jesus was crucified, God abolished the need for the temple in Jerusalem, tearing the curtain that separated the Most Holy from His people to demonstrate that His presence would no longer be found inside a building. God's presence now resides in the very people who belong to Him because they have been reconciled to God through faith in Jesus Christ. God showed this to John in the book of Revelation: "Behold, the tabernacle of God is with men, and He will dwell with them, and they shall be His people. God Himself will be with them and be their God" (21:3). There is no longer a need for a temple, simply because *we* are His temple!

God's people are unified through their obedience.

The devil divides. He works ceaselessly to separate what God has brought together: marriages, churches, any relationship where unity and commitment are essential. Ironically, the devil also works tirelessly to *remove* separations and divisions that God has established: right from wrong, darkness from light, good from evil, and on and on. The evil one's goal is to create unity in wickedness and disunity in righteousness.

It is interesting to note that the nations of Israel and Judah were fairly unified in pursuing wickedness for many generations, but this was the sort of unity that the devil breeds, not the unity that God requires. The Lord calls His people to be unified together in obedience; when we pursue disobedience, or when we allow disunity to separate Christians, we are following the paths of wickedness rather than the ways of righteousness.

The exiles who returned to Jerusalem drew together with one accord, working together as one to reestablish godly worship—and the Lord blessed their efforts tremendously. We will see clearly as we go through these studies how the Lord stymied the efforts of others who sought to disrupt His work, and how He preserved and blessed His people as they did that work. When Christians unite in obedience to God's Word, nothing can stand in their way.

The Lord will put an end to mourning.

As the returning exiles laid the foundation for the temple in Jerusalem, there was a very mixed response from the people. Many shouted with joy at seeing the Lord rebuilding what had been destroyed, while many others wept with deep grief over their memories of what had once been. Ironically, both responses were valid—but in the long run, the joyful shouting drowned out the tears.

The people of Israel had good reason to mourn, since it was their own sin and stubbornness that brought about the destruction of the temple and the loss of all it contained—including the ark of the covenant. Yet God had not abandoned His people, and He had not forgotten His promises of faithfulness and blessing. The Lord was still at work, and what mattered most was that Israel still existed, kept by the promise of God. Tears had a place, but the shouts of joy would last far longer.

When we sin, we often do grave damage to ourselves and others. We do well when we grieve and mourn over our own sinful behavior, repenting and recognizing the damage we've caused. But we must also remember that God has not abandoned us, even in the midst of deliberate sin. He may choose to bring discipline into our lives to urge us toward repentance, but He will never forsake us and will never disinherit those who are His children through the redemption of Jesus Christ. In the eternal kingdom, "God will wipe away every tear from their eyes; there shall be no more death, nor sorrow, nor crying. There shall be no more pain, for the former things have passed away" (Revelation 21:4).

✌ DIGGING DEEPER ✌

5. *Why did some people shout with joy when the foundation was laid? Why did others weep? If you'd been there, how would you have responded?*

6. If you had been outside Jerusalem at the time of this loud shouting, how would you have reacted to the noise? How does your worship of God influence the people around you?

7. Why was unity among the people so important to rebuilding the temple? In what ways is unity among Christians important today?

8. What does the Bible mean when it says that a Christian is the temple of God? What implications does this have in your own life?

9. When have you grieved over your past sins? When have you rejoiced over God's faithfulness and blessings? When has He turned your tears into joy?

10. Which takes higher priority in your life: personal obedience to God's Word, or regular attendance at church? Which is God's highest priority?

~ 3 ~
FACING OPPOSITION

EZRA 4

↰ HISTORICAL BACKGROUND ↰

In 722 BC, the Assyrians invaded Israel and carried away the northern tribes into captivity. They then began to repopulate the area around Samaria, Israel's former capital, with people from other, distant lands that they had conquered. Those foreigners settled in Samaria and intermarried with the few Israelites who were still living there, and their descendants became known as Samaritans.

These Samaritans did not fear God, and the Lord sent wild lions as a form of discipline. The people recognized this as the hand of God, but they thought He was only the god of Samaria; they did not understand that His control extends to the entire world. So the Lord sent a priest to live with them, and he "taught them how they should fear the LORD" (2 Kings 17:28). The Samaritans embraced the worship rituals that the priest taught, but they did not forsake their other gods; they thought they could simply add the God of all creation to their long list of idols, and invented their own syncretistic religious practices.

When Zerubbabel and the people of Judah returned to Jerusalem, they found that the Samaritans were still living nearby. In this study, we will see what happens when obedient believers are confronted by pious frauds.

↰ READING EZRA 4:1–24 ↰

A FRIENDLY OFFER: *The Samaritans, neighbors of the Jews, come to Jerusalem and offer to help build God's temple. But the people of Judah reject the offer.*

1. THE ADVERSARIES OF JUDAH AND BENJAMIN: These were the Samaritans. When Assyria carried the nation of Israel into captivity, the land was resettled with people from other lands in and around Samaria. Those foreigners had intermarried with the remaining Israelites, and brought their own brands of idolatry with them.

2. WE SEEK YOUR GOD AS YOU DO: This statement was true from the Samaritans' point of view, but it was absolutely false from God's perspective. The Lord had sent a priest to Samaria to teach His truth to those who had been transported there by the Assyrians after the Israelite captivity. They had embraced the Lord in part, thinking that He was "the God of the land" (2 Kings 17:26) to which they had been transported, and they wanted to appease Him. But they had not forsaken their false gods in the process; they had merely attempted to add the one true God to their pantheon of idols.

3. WE ALONE WILL BUILD TO THE LORD GOD OF ISRAEL: This was an important and costly decision on the part of Judah's leaders. They were not arbitrarily excluding outsiders from building the temple out of some spirit of snobbery; nor were they excluding others merely out of obedience to Cyrus's commands. They were taking a firm stand that only God's obedient worshipers were permitted to participate in building His temple, and they were avoiding contact with the very idolatry that had caused the Lord to send them into captivity in the first place.

SHOWING THEIR TRUE FACE: *The Samaritans respond by showing their true motives as they begin an ongoing attempt to stop God's work in Jerusalem.*

4. TRIED TO DISCOURAGE THE PEOPLE OF JUDAH: Discouragement is one of the devil's favorite tactics in trying to thwart the work of God. His goal is to persuade God's people to give up on obedience and turn to the easier temptations of the flesh. God warns against giving in to discouragement (Deuteronomy 1:21). He wants us to choose instead to trust Him for the outcome.

5. HIRED COUNSELORS AGAINST THEM: The Samaritans evidently took some form of legal action against the Jews, hoping to bog them down in litigation if they couldn't prevent the rebuilding outright. God's enemies still use this tactic today, attempting to thwart the spread of the gospel through laws and lawsuits.

ALL THE DAYS OF CYRUS: This opposition continued for fifteen to twenty years.

6. THEY WROTE AN ACCUSATION: The Hebrew word for "accusation" here is related to the word for "Satan." Satan is the accuser of the brethren (Revelation 12:10), the one who tirelessly brings accusations against God's people. The enemies of God's people are of their father, the devil (John 8:44), and thus persistently do the same.

7. ARTAXERXES KING OF PERSIA: This occurred later, during the time when Nehemiah was ministering in Jerusalem. We will learn more of this in future studies.

10. THE GREAT AND NOBLE OSNAPPER: This is probably another name for the Assyrian king who resettled Samaria with foreigners. The obsequious tone of the enemies' letter to Artaxerxes is typical of those who use flattery and attempt to ingratiate themselves to those in power, in hopes of accomplishing their own personal agendas. The Assyrians were noted for their cruelty and barbarity, and their kings were anything but "great and noble."

12. THE REBELLIOUS AND EVIL CITY: God's view of Jerusalem was quite different: "Beautiful in elevation, the joy of the whole earth, is Mount Zion on the sides of the north, the city of the great King" (Psalm 48:2). Yet here is another favorite tactic of God's enemies, to accuse His people of the very wickedness that they commit themselves. "Woe to those who call evil good, and good evil; who put darkness for light, and light for darkness; who put bitter for sweet, and sweet for bitter!" (Isaiah 5:20).

SPEAKING THE KING'S LANGUAGE: *The enemies of God finally find a sympathetic ear with King Artaxerxes—when they tell him that he'll lose money—and he stops the work.*

13. THEY WILL NOT PAY TAX, TRIBUTE, OR CUSTOM: This, of course, was not true, yet the accusation undoubtedly hit a chord in the mind of King Artaxerxes. Judah had historically refused to pay tribute to foreign kings prior to the captivity.

THE KING'S TREASURY WILL BE DIMINISHED: But here is the crux of their real argument: if King Artaxerxes permitted the Jews to continue their rebuilding projects, he would lose money. Rulers in Ezra's day were no different from those in our own time, and this argument proved all too effective.

14. IT WAS NOT PROPER FOR US TO SEE THE KING'S DISHONOR: Here again we see the hypocrisy and dissembling of God's enemies, pretending that they have high and lofty motives, yet pursuing their own selfish gain.

19. REBELLION AND SEDITION HAVE BEEN FOSTERED IN IT: This refers to the rebellions of Kings Jehoiakim (2 Kings 24:1), Jehoiachin (2 Kings 24:12), and Zedekiah (2 Kings 24:20)—all of whom ruled in Judah prior to the captivity. It is worth noting, however, that these rebellions were against Babylon, not against Persia.

23. BY FORCE OF ARMS MADE THEM CEASE: The enemies of God's people may succeed temporarily in outlawing obedience to His Word, but God is always in control, and no power on earth or in hell can prevent the fulfillment of His plans. In Study 8, we will see that the temple eventually was completed in spite of God's enemies.

↪ First Impressions ↩

1. If you had been present when the Samaritans offered to help, how would you have responded? Why did the Jews reject their offer?

2. The Samaritans told the Jews, "We seek your God as you do" (v. 2). In what ways was this partially true? In what ways was it false? Why did it matter?

3. What tactics did the Samaritans use to discourage the people of Judah? When have you faced similar opposition?

4. *How did the Samaritans use Persia's political and legal system to persecute God's peo-ple? Why were they opposed to the temple's construction? Why was that an effective way to oppose God's work?*

⤳ Some Key Principles ⤳

One cannot serve God and other "gods" at the same time.

The people of Samaria had been taught the truths of God's Words, and they understood (at least outwardly) the proper worship of Yahweh. They even embraced that worship, making sacrifices to God on a regular basis. The problem was that they did not renounce their false gods in the process. They hoped to placate the true God while not repenting of their idolatry. To the casual observer they might have appeared as worshipers of Yahweh, but they did not obey His command to turn away from false gods—and God does not share His glory with any mythical pantheon.

People still make this mistake today. Many of them have been instructed in the truths of God's Word, and they may even regularly attend a church that purports to be "Christian"—but church attendance will not bring salvation. You must *serve God* and God alone—not both God and the flesh. Jesus was very clear on this: "No one can serve two masters; for either he will hate the one and love the other, or else he will be loyal to the one and despise the other. You cannot serve God and mammon" (Matthew 6:24). (Mammon refers to the love of material possessions and comforts, but this is only one of the many forms of idolatry in which people engage today.)

Another trap the devil uses is syncretism, where people attempt to commingle elements of many different religions into their own personal brand of worship. This, too, is very common today, as people attempt to amalgamate many contradictory religious systems into their own notions of "transcendence." Even some who purport to teach God's Word are adulterating it with worldly notions of evolution, psychology, and many other false teachings. But Jesus stated very clearly, "I am the way, the truth, and the life. No one comes to the Father except through Me" (John 14:6). There is no other way to salvation than through Jesus Christ, and the Lord will not tolerate any adulteration of His Word.

The devil wears many disguises.

The Samaritans approached the leaders of Judah with a friendly offer to help them build the temple. They even pointed out that they all worshiped the same God, and therefore they should be working together toward their common goal. To refuse such kindness would be rude at best, a refusal to get along with others, even a self-righteous hypocrisy—yet that is precisely what God's people did: they refused to permit the Samaritans to participate in the work that God had given them.

This refusal, however, was not self-righteousness or rudeness; it was a recognition that the evil one was behind the offer. The Jews did not judge the Samaritans' hearts; they simply compared their behavior with God's revelation and recognized that the Samaritans did not worship God as He commanded them to. That was enough to cause Judah to reject their offer, whatever spirit lay behind it. Subsequent events proved that the offer was made in a spirit of duplicity. The Samaritans were pretending to be friendly while actually being sinister. Solomon warned of such people when he wrote, "Faithful are the wounds of a friend, but the kisses of an enemy are deceitful" (Proverbs 27:6).

Paul further warned us, "Satan himself transforms himself into an angel of light. Therefore it is no great thing if his ministers also transform themselves into ministers of righteousness, whose end will be according to their works" (2 Corinthians 11:14–15). In other words, Christians must be on guard against those who pretend to be godly but are not, because there are many who try to "transform themselves into ministers of righteousness" by wearing a false disguise. Jesus warned us, "Behold, I send you out as sheep in the midst of wolves. Therefore be wise as serpents and harmless as doves" (Matthew 10:16)—be always aware of the ways of the evil one without ever practicing those tactics yourself. Christians should never practice hypocrisy or false pretense, while always remembering that the devil does.

God commands us to resist discouragement.

The enemies of God's people attempted to interrupt their works of obedience by causing them to become discouraged. The King James Version renders verse 4, "The people of the land weakened the hands of the people of Judah," and this captures the essence of discouragement: to become weak, to sink down, to lose the ability to carry on, and to let God's projects drop from despair.

Fear is at the root of discouragement. You are faced with a circumstance that is beyond your control, and suddenly you begin to fear that it's beyond God's control as well. And if it's beyond God's control, you might as well give up now—which is, of course, precisely what Satan is hoping for. But God commands us not to give in to fear, but to strengthen our hands when they become weak (Hebrews 12:12; cf. Isaiah 41:10). The best way to do this, wrote the author of Hebrews, is to "consider Him who endured such hostility from sinners against Himself, lest you become weary and discouraged in your souls" (12:3). Remember that Jesus Himself faced immense opposition—more severe than any we will ever face—and He overcame all through the faithfulness of God and through utter confidence in and reliance upon His sovereignty.

⤳ Digging Deeper ⤶

5. *Why were the Samaritans not qualified to participate in the work of building the temple? What was wrong with their worship of God? Why are such matters important to God?*

6. *What is the difference between discerning false motives and judging other people? What does it mean to be "wise as serpents and harmless as doves"? How is this done?*

7. How is discouragement related to fear? How is fear related to faith? What is the solution to discouragement? What role do a person's deliberate choices play?

8. What elements of syncretism (blending false religions with God's Word) are being taught today? How can a Christian discern such false teachings?

9. Is someone or something discouraging you from doing the will of God? How can the example of Jesus give you courage and perseverance? What can other Christians do to help?

10. Are you trying to serve two masters? What is competing with your loyalty to Christ? What will you do to remove that from your life?

REBUILDING THE WALL

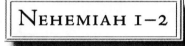

⤳ HISTORICAL BACKGROUND ⤳

We now move forward in time approximately one hundred years to 446 BC, when a man named Nehemiah was serving King Artaxerxes of Persia. Nehemiah held a very important post in the king's court as his personal cupbearer, or "food taster." He was responsible to ensure that the king did not ingest any poison, which was a fairly common way of assassinating an unpopular monarch in that time. For Nehemiah, this position came with a great degree of trust and intimacy with the king, and probably brought great wealth, comfort, and influence at court as well.

Meanwhile, the Jews who went to Jerusalem with Zerubbabel (and their descendants) were struggling against opposition and hatred from their enemies. The rebuilding project had been halted when enemies of the Jews persuaded King Artaxerxes to forbid completion of the city wall, the most important part of defense for not only the temple but the people themselves.

Judah was far away from Susa, Persia's capital city, where Nehemiah served the king, and it took a full three months to travel between the two cities. Yet when Nehemiah learned of the Jews' plight, he immediately made plans to forsake his comfortable situation and go join his people in their work to rebuild the wall—even at great cost to himself.

⤳ READING NEHEMIAH 1:1–11 ⤳

MOURNING WITH THE MOURNERS: *Nehemiah, the king's cupbearer, learns of the situation in Jerusalem, and responds in deep grief.*

1. NEHEMIAH: Nehemiah was the cupbearer to King Artaxerxes of Persia. His name means "Yahweh comforts."

THE TWENTIETH YEAR: November–December 446 BC.

Shushan the citadel: Also known as Susa, located east of Babylon, approximately 150 miles north of the Persian Gulf. The book of Esther took place in this city, not long before the events of Nehemiah, and Esther may well have been still alive.

3. in great distress and reproach: In Study 3, we saw some of the distress and reproach suffered by the Jews in Jerusalem as they experienced the betrayal and opposition of the Samaritans. Yet their suffering was greater than mere human opposition. In Nehemiah's day, pagans thought that a god's strength was reflected by the walls and fortifications that surrounded his temple. The lack of city walls reflected badly upon the character of God in the eyes of Judah's neighbors, and it also left the temple unprotected against further attacks and desecration.

4. I sat down and wept: Nehemiah was deeply moved by the plight of his fellow Jews in Jerusalem. He did far more than express shallow sympathy; he reacted as though he were right there, suffering with them.

fasting and praying: Nehemiah's mourning and grief were not impotent; he did not sit in Persia's palace, wringing his hands. He took action to help those who were suffering, and he began with the most important and effective step: he went before the Lord in prayer and fasting, seeking His will and intervention.

Responding with Prayer: *Nehemiah does more than sit and weep—he goes before God and asks for His help and guidance.*

---

5. You who keep Your covenant and mercy: In this beautiful prayer, Nehemiah revealed an important fact concerning God's character: He is completely faithful to His promises. The people of Jerusalem didn't need any walls to protect the temple or themselves; they were shielded by God's complete faithfulness (although it was still God's will that the walls be rebuilt). Nehemiah also recognized God's absolute sovereignty over all the affairs of mankind—He is the "Lord God of heaven," and He rules in the lives of kings and paupers alike.

6. I pray . . . day and night: Nehemiah prayed persistently over a period of days, not simply on this one occasion.

the children of Israel . . . my father's house and I: Notice the progression of Nehemiah's confession. He acknowledged first that his nation had sinned against the Lord, forsaking Him and pursuing false gods. He then confessed that his "father's house" had not been faithful to the Lord, encompassing his family and those for whom he was responsible. (This might be comparable to praying for one's immediate family and local church in modern times.) Finally, he acknowledged that he was personally guilty of sin and failure before the Lord, not omitting his own areas of culpability but recognizing that his own sinful nature contributed to the unfaithfulness of his tribe and nation. When one begins by focusing on God's faithful and holy nature, recognition of sin—both personal and corporate—naturally follows.

8. REMEMBER, I PRAY: Nehemiah was asking the Lord to act on His promises, not suggesting that He had forgotten something. The Lord loves to have us quote His Word, not in an accusatory way, but in an expectant way, indicating that we have read His promises and that we have faith that He will keep them. And He always does.

9. I WILL GATHER THEM FROM THERE: As we have already seen, the Lord had promised His people that He would scatter them to the four winds if they refused to heed His Word (Deuteronomy 4:25–28), and He had kept this promise. He had also promised that, at the end of seventy years, He would gather a remnant and return them to His chosen city of Jerusalem (vv. 29–31). The imagery used here is of sowing seed (which was scattered randomly by hand) and reaping a harvest. The Lord had scattered His people when they were unfaithful, but He had reaped a harvest of obedient, loving children.

11. THE KING'S CUPBEARER: Nehemiah held one of the most trusted and intimate positions in Persia. His job was to ensure the king's safety by personally tasting his food first, to be certain that no one poisoned him. This situation provided Nehemiah with a unique opportunity to speak confidentially with the king, and that was what he was preparing to do as he prayed and fasted. ("This man" refers to the king, whom Nehemiah was about to petition.)

⤝ READING NEHEMIAH 2:1–20 ⤞

....

PREPARING TO APPROACH THE KING: *Nehemiah next determines to ask the king for a leave of absence—but this was a very dangerous request to make.*

1. THE MONTH OF NISAN: March–April 445 BC, approximately four months since Nehemiah first learned of the situation in Jerusalem (1:1).

I TOOK THE WINE AND GAVE IT TO THE KING: This was Nehemiah's chief responsibility, ensuring that the king's enemies did not poison him. It also established a bond of trust between him and Artaxerxes, as Nehemiah placed his own life on the line every time he sampled the king's food and drink. This was a strategic moment for him to speak with the king, while carrying out his duties and risking his life for his king.

I HAD NEVER BEEN SAD IN HIS PRESENCE: Court etiquette in ancient times required that subjects appear cheerful before their king, and a sad or grim countenance could bring down the royal wrath (cf. Esther 4:2). Happy subjects suggested that the king was a good and wise ruler, while tears suggested otherwise. As cupbearer, Nehemiah would have needed to observe such customs of courtly behavior very carefully.

2. SINCE YOU ARE NOT SICK: The king might have been referring to Nehemiah's general state of health (which is the usual understanding here), but he might also have been suggesting that Nehemiah had clearly not ingested poison from the king's cup and therefore should be pleased. Middle Eastern monarchs in general did not take time to consider the personal lives of their subjects.

I BECAME DREADFULLY AFRAID: Nehemiah actually had good reason to be afraid, from a human standpoint. As already stated, it was very risky business to appear unhappy in the presence of the king. But even more than that, Nehemiah was planning to request permission to leave the king's service, which would have been seen as a terrible insult from someone who held such a high and trusted position. He was also going to ask to rebuild the walls of Jerusalem from the very king who had ordered the building to stop. But Nehemiah was not acting from a human perspective; he knew that the Lord had control over the king's decisions (Proverbs 21:1).

4. So I PRAYED TO THE GOD OF HEAVEN: Nehemiah was a man of prayer. He had fasted and prayed for several days prior to making his request to the king, but even in the midst of taking action, he was speaking to the Lord.

6. THE QUEEN ALSO SITTING BESIDE HIM: Esther had been queen of King Ahasuerus (Xerxes), who was King Artaxerxes' father. It is possible that her role as the present king's stepmother made him predisposed to show favor to the Jews—particularly if she was still alive at the time.

WHATEVER YOU NEED: *The Lord moves the king's heart to grant his request for a trip to Judah, and he gives him much more, besides.*

---

7. LET LETTERS BE GIVEN TO ME: These letters would bear the royal seal of Artaxerxes, commanding all government officials to assist Nehemiah on his trip to Judah and his work in Jerusalem. The king was thus giving Nehemiah full authority as one of his officials in Judah.

8. HE MUST GIVE ME TIMBER: In addition to governing authority and safe passage, the king also provided much of the raw material needed to rebuild the city gates and wall—and Nehemiah's own house as well. Lumber was a precious commodity, and forests were carefully guarded.

ACCORDING TO THE GOOD HAND OF MY GOD UPON ME: Nehemiah was undoubtedly grateful to King Artaxerxes for his generosity, but he recognized the more important fact that his success was due solely to God's sovereign hand. It was the Lord who moved the king's heart, even after Artaxerxes had previously forbidden any such reconstruction projects in Jerusalem.

9. THE KING HAD SENT CAPTAINS OF THE ARMY AND HORSEMEN: This was a wise human precaution. It was a two-month journey from Susa to Jerusalem, and the roads along the way were fraught with banditry. The letters Nehemiah carried bore the king's seal, and as such were immensely valuable because they conferred upon the bearer the full authority of the king of Persia. That alone would have put Nehemiah's life in extreme peril on such a long journey, to say nothing of the many peoples along the way who were enemies of the Jews. Yet from God's perspective, a military guard was merely superfluous; He had determined that Nehemiah should go to Jerusalem, and no power on earth could have prevented his safe arrival.

MORE OPPOSITION: *Initiating the project of rebuilding is merely a beginning, and Satan's agents will continue to oppose God's work at every step.*

10. SANBALLAT . . . AND TOBIAH: Sanballat was governor of Samaria, and was probably also a Moabite—an ancient enemy of Israel. Tobiah was governor of the region east of the Jordan River, and he was an Ammonite—another ancient enemy of God's people. These two men were probably also behind the opposition against Zerubbabel that had previously stopped the work in Jerusalem (Study 3).

DISTURBED THAT A MAN HAD COME: This attitude revealed the true nature of these men and their cohorts: they were committed enemies of God and His people. It is particularly revealing that they were not so much opposed to the authority that Nehemiah wielded; they were specifically opposed to anyone who sought "the well-being of the children of Israel."

12. I TOLD NO ONE: Nehemiah needed to know specifically what condition the wall was in, where it needed most immediate attention, what would be required, and so forth. He chose to gain this information in secret because he knew that his enemies were watching him, and he didn't know yet who could be trusted. He probably suspected that even some of the Jews in the city were in league with Sanballat and Tobiah, and to be safe he did not even tell "the Jews, the priests, the nobles, the officials, or the others who did the work" (v. 16) what he was doing.

17. LET US BUILD: Nehemiah next invited all of God's people to join him in the work. It was not Nehemiah's project; it was God's project, and the Lord calls all His children to be involved in His work. This also would enable Nehemiah to discover who was fully committed to the plans of God, as those would be the people who threw themselves into the rebuilding. Those who held back for some reason would remain under his suspicions of duplicity.

THAT WE MAY NO LONGER BE A REPROACH: Here is Nehemiah's motivation in undertaking this huge project: he was concerned about the glory of God. The destruction of the temple and city of Jerusalem made a mockery of God's name in the eyes of Judah's enemies, so Nehemiah called upon the people of God to restore His glory to the world around them.

18. I TOLD THEM OF THE HAND OF MY GOD: It is good to tell others of the ways God has blessed you and how you have seen Him working faithfully in your own life. This encourages others who might be facing discouragement, and it brings glory to His name.

ᔕ FIRST IMPRESSIONS ᔓ

1. *Why was Nehemiah so upset when he learned of the plight of the Jews in Jerusalem? What was his response?*

2. *What was the "great distress and reproach" that the Jews were facing in Judah? In what ways did this reflect on God's glory?*

3. Why did Nehemiah take stock of the wall around Jerusalem in secret? Why did he then call all the people to join him in the rebuilding? What does his example teach about leadership?

4. Take time to consider the elements of Nehemiah's prayer (1:5–11). What can you learn about prayer from his example?

✒ Some Key Principles ✒

Service is crucial, especially when it's costly.

Nehemiah lived in Persia, the greatest and wealthiest nation of its day. Furthermore, he lived in Susa, the nation's capital and one of the richest and most comfortable of the Persian cities. To top this off, he was the cupbearer to the king himself, a position of high trust and influence. He was undoubtedly a rich and influential man, high in the ranks of the most powerful nation on earth. Meanwhile, Jerusalem was very far away—a journey of two full months, and very easy to forget about.

Yet, when Nehemiah heard about the plight of his fellow Jews in far-off Judah, he mourned, wept, fasted, and prayed. What's more, he determined in his heart to forsake all the blessings and comforts of Persia, exchanging them willingly for hard work, rough living conditions, and constant hatred and opposition from God's enemies. In fact, Nehemiah was so determined to help with the work in Jerusalem that he risked his own life to get there, putting himself in peril of the king's wrath as well as making the dangerous and uncomfortable trip to Judah.

It was not wrong or sinful for Nehemiah to enjoy the comforts of Persia and the king's court; the Lord had placed him in his position, and he was being faithful to the tasks God gave him. But the Lord had placed him there specifically so that he might be positioned to help the Jews at this moment of crisis, just as He had placed Esther where she could save the Jews from annihilation a generation earlier (Esther 4:14). The Lord was calling upon Nehemiah to voluntarily forsake all these blessings in order to participate in an important project, but the blessings that came from his obedience far surpassed all the comforts of the king's palace. If the Lord calls you in a similar way to forsake your comfort for the sake of His work, heed the call! You will bring glory to His name, and great blessings to yourself.

Our protection is found in God alone.

The Jews in Jerusalem were anxious to rebuild the city walls as a strong defense against the many enemies who surrounded them and would have been glad to see them carried off into captivity once again. King Artaxerxes provided Nehemiah with a powerful military escort to protect him on the dangerous journey from Susa to Jerusalem, a trip that posed threats to Nehemiah's life from many sources, human and natural. These were dangerous times for the Jews, as there were many who hated them and longed to participate in their destruction.

Yet the Lord did not need stone walls or well-armed soldiers to protect His people. His omnipotent hand was sufficient, and His faithfulness to His promises ensured that nothing could touch His servants without His permission. Ezra had made the same two-month journey previously without any military escort, deliberately choosing to trust in the Lord's protection (Ezra 8:22)—and his faith proved sound. This does not mean, of course, that Nehemiah had less faith than Ezra; the king had offered the escort, and Nehemiah saw that as God's provision at the time. Nevertheless, had the king *not* offered any soldiers, Nehemiah would still have arrived safely through the Lord's faithfulness.

However, we must not overlook the important element of obedience in the Lord's protection. Notice what Nehemiah prayed in 1:5: "O great and awesome God, You who keep Your covenant and mercy with those who love You and observe Your commandments . . ." The Lord is always faithful to His promises, faithful to protect His children from the enemy, but He also expects us to be faithful to His Word. When we sin, we make ourselves vulnerable to the attacks of the evil one, and we hinder God's hand of blessing in our lives. Our job is to obey His Word and trust Him for our needs.

God loves to see the faith of His people.

When Nehemiah spent time in fasting and prayer, prior to approaching the king with his risky request, he reminded God of the promises He'd made concerning Judah. He pointed out in prayer that the Lord had kept His promise to send the people into captivity if they persisted in idolatry, and he then reminded Him of His further promise to return them to Judah after seventy years. He was reminding the Lord of these things, not out of a spirit of accusation, but in a spirit of expectation: seventy years had expired, and Nehemiah fully expected that the Lord would fulfill His promise to return the Jews to Judah.

There is another layer to this prayer, however, which we might easily overlook: in order for Nehemiah to remind God of His promises, he had to know those promises in the first place. Nehemiah's knowledge of the seventy-year limitation on the captivity indicated that he had spent time reading and meditating on the Word of God. This is one reason why the Lord is pleased when we quote His Word to Him in prayer, because He wants us to read it, memorize it, and meditate on it. But He also wants us to make His Word part of our own lives, to ask ourselves how it applies to each of us personally in our daily routines.

Reminding the Lord of His promises delights Him, and it is good for us. He will keep His promises anyway, of course, simply because He never fails—yet the Lord delights in His children reminding Him of His Word, because it shows that we have faith in His character, faith in His faithfulness. It also strengthens us when we remind *ourselves* of His promises, deepening our faith and strengthening weak hands.

⌁ Digging Deeper ⌁

5. *What risks did Nehemiah take to help the Jews in Judah? Why did he do this? What motivated him? What would you have done in his situation?*

6. *Why did Ezra not take a military escort on his trip to Judah (Ezra 8:22)? Why did Nehemiah accept the king's guard on his trip? What do these men's attitudes reveal about God's protection? about our faith?*

7. Why did Nehemiah remind God of His promises in his prayer? What effect might this have had on Nehemiah? on God? How do these principles apply to your prayer life?

8. What specifically did Nehemiah tell the people in Jerusalem (2:18)? Why? How did they respond? How might these insights apply to your witness for Christ?

9.   What are you presently depending upon for your security: Your job? Retirement bene-
     fits? Health insurance? In what areas might you need to place more faith in God's
     protection?

10. When has another Christian served you at great cost to him- or herself? Why did he
     or she do so? Whom might the Lord be calling you to serve this week?

~ 5 ~
FACING MORE OPPOSITION

(Acre) Akko
(Haifa)Hefa
Nazerat-Irbid
Az Zar
Amman
(Bethlehem)

NEHEMIAH 4

⌁ HISTORICAL BACKGROUND ⌁

Nehemiah has been in Jerusalem for some time now, and the Jews have been working on the walls and gates with great vigor and zeal. Through the Lord's blessing and help, they have made good progress, and the wall itself is nearly half built.

But the Jews' enemies have not been idle either. In this chapter, we will see that their opposition to the Lord's work has increased with as much zeal and vigor as the Jews have shown. And they will stop at nothing to prevent God's work from being completed, resorting to all forms of verbal abuse and scandal—all the way to planning a mass murder of the Jews.

Nehemiah, however, demonstrates that God's people must expect opposition, and we must always be prepared to face it. The most important lesson we will see from this opposition is that you should trust in God's promises as you accomplish the tasks which He has given you.

⌁ READING NEHEMIAH 4:1–23 ⌁

MOCKERY AND DISDAIN: *The enemies of God's people learn of the plan to rebuild the walls, and they are filled with fury.*

1. IT SO HAPPENED: The immense project of rebuilding the walls and gates had begun. See Nehemiah 3 for a detailed list of all the aspects of construction and the people who undertook it.

FURIOUS AND VERY INDIGNANT: On the surface, Sanballat was outraged by the fact that the Jews had overridden his authority in the region by gaining the support of the king. But the deeper fact is that he was an enemy of God, and therefore an enemy of God's people. He could not abide the thought that the Jews were going to prosper and rebuild their beloved city of Jerusalem.

2. HE SPOKE BEFORE HIS BRETHREN: To have any effect, mockery requires a sympathetic audience, so Sanballat attempted to draw others into his mockery of the Jews. His "brethren" would have been others of like mind who also hated God's people, and his inclusion of the army probably indicates that he hoped to incite violence against them.

4. HEAR, O OUR GOD: Once again, Nehemiah's first response to danger and opposition was to bow before the Lord in prayer. Notice that Nehemiah did not respond to the taunts and mockery of his enemies; instead, he poured out his heart to the Lord and allowed Him to deal with the opposition.

5. DO NOT COVER THEIR INIQUITY: Nehemiah was acknowledging that his enemies were attacking God rather than him; it was God whom they despised, and Nehemiah was calling upon the Lord to defend His glory before the world. Nehemiah recognized that forgiveness is granted, not to those who oppose the will of God, but to those who eagerly submit to His will.

6. SO WE BUILT THE WALL: Nehemiah effectively turned the situation over to the Lord in his short prayer, and then he returned his focus to the work that the Lord had given him. He did not pretend that the opposition did not exist; he turned to God in prayer and continued working on the wall trusting that God would ultimately be their defender.

THE PEOPLE HAD A MIND TO WORK: During the early phases of the building project, the people were enthusiastic and eager to participate. They were excited to see the progress as the wall came together, but human nature tends to cause us to lose enthusiasm as time passes. It is then that a believer's determination becomes important in obeying and completing the Lord's work. As enthusiasm dissipates, distractions and discouragement multiply.

ENEMIES ON ALL SIDES: *People band together on all four sides of Jerusalem to hinder God's work—people who would ordinarily not be allies with one another.*

7. THE ARABS, THE AMMONITES, AND THE ASHDODITES: Sanballat represented the Samaritans to the north; the Arabs were located to the south; the Ammonites (with Tobiah) were to the east; and the Ashdodites were located to the west—thus effectively surrounding the people of God on every side. Ironically, these groups of people would never have cooperated together under normal circumstances; what drew them together in this alliance was a mutual hatred of God and His people. This same trend can be seen today in the Middle East.

THEY BECAME VERY ANGRY: Here the enemies tipped their hand, showing the true nature of their opposition. They had pretended to care about the king's taxes and about national security, and acted as if the Jews could not construct anything lasting—but in the end they were only angry at the thought of the Jews being able to defend themselves. God's enemies criticize, manipulate, and persecute God's people today just as they did then.

8. CREATE CONFUSION: This is another of the devil's favorite tactics, creating confusion and chaos wherever unity exists among God's people. It is not uncommon for the people of God to be tempted toward disunity, especially during times of critical work on behalf of the Lord. The enemies of the Jews did not care what the people believed; they simply wanted to stop work on the wall.

9. WE MADE OUR PRAYER . . . WE SET A WATCH: Note the twofold approach to the danger they faced: they turned to God in prayer, and they took steps to guard themselves. The Jews recognized that their protection was from God alone, yet that did not exempt them from carrying out their basic human responsibilities. It would have been negligent not to establish watchmen to guard the wall (and their homes) at night. The Lord wants His children to trust Him for their security, but He also expects them to be responsible.

DISCOURAGEMENT AND VIOLENCE: *God's enemies now resort to threats of murder, and the Jews begin to grow weary and discouraged.*

10. THE STRENGTH OF THE LABORERS IS FAILING: The Jews' initial enthusiasm had worn off, and fatigue was setting in. This is a natural human tendency when undertaking any large project, and facing strong opposition from God's enemies only increases the process, leading to discouragement and a desire to quit. It is at this point when God's people need to deliberately draw strength from the Lord through prayer and meditation on His Word. This process may also require practical steps, as demonstrated in the following verses.

SO MUCH RUBBISH: This would have been debris from the original wall, rubble left behind by the Babylonian army when they tore it down.

11. KILL THEM AND CAUSE THE WORK TO CEASE: God's enemies will stop at nothing, even mass murder, in hopes of preventing the fulfillment of His plans. This is a futile hope, however, as nothing whatsoever can prevent God's plans from coming to pass. The destruction His enemies plan will come upon their own heads (Proverbs 26:27).

12. the Jews who dwelt near them: These were Jews who had not gotten involved in the rebuilding project. They probably meant well, intending to warn the others of an impending attack, but they had become tools of the enemies, yielding to fear and potentially spreading that fear to the people who were actually working. Fear is the enemy of God's people.

Foiled Again: *The Lord prevents His enemies from attacking His people during the work of rebuilding, for the battle belongs to Him alone.*

14. Do not be afraid of them: The Scripture often repeats this important injunction, calling God's people to deliberately choose not to yield to fear, because fear leads one away from God rather than toward Him.

Remember the Lord . . . and fight: Here again we see Nehemiah's approach, both spiritual and practical. Remembering the Lord involves meditating on His Word and His character, as well as turning to Him in prayer. The fighting that Nehemiah had in mind was quite literal, as demonstrated by the Jews' willingness to take up arms to defend themselves against attack.

15. God had brought their plot to nothing: Nehemiah never lost sight of the fact that God was in control of all events. The plot was not foiled because the Jews had learned about it, nor because of their readiness to fight back—it was foiled because God prevented it.

16. held the spears, the shields, the bows, and wore armor: Notice that half of these weapons are offensive (spears and bows), and half are defensive (shields and armor). Paul used such military weaponry to describe the Christian life, including the shield of faith, the breastplate of righteousness, and "the sword of the Spirit, which is the word of God" (Ephesians 6:14–17). Yet on a very practical level, Nehemiah took strong precautions to guard against the threatened physical attack of the enemy, dividing the workers into two teams: one to guard while the other one worked.

18. the one who sounded the trumpet: The trumpet would have sounded a loud call to arms, alerting all the Jews of an attack. Nehemiah took it upon himself, as the Lord's appointed leader of this project, to stand guard vigilantly on behalf of those under his leadership.

20. Our God will fight for us: Once again, Nehemiah reminded his co-workers that the battle belonged to the Lord, not to the strength of their arms.

✦ First Impressions ✦

1. Why were the enemies of the Jews "furious and very indignant" (v. 1) about their building the wall? What enraged them? With whom were they angry?

2. What tactics did the enemies use to thwart the rebuilding project? How do God's enemies today use similar tactics?

3. Why did Nehemiah command his workers to go around armed? What effect did this probably have on the work? What effect did it have on the enemies?

4. *What role did prayer play in the events of this chapter? What practical steps did the people take? How does a Christian blend prayer and practical common sense?*

☙ Some Key Principles ☙

Expect opposition, but don't ignore it.

Zerubbabel, Ezra, and Nehemiah all faced determined opposition from powerful foes, yet each persisted in doing the Lord's work. They understood that life is filled with spiritual battles, as the enemy of our souls continuously strives to hinder the work of God. These men expected opposition to the Lord's great project of rebuilding Jerusalem, and they were not caught off guard when it came.

At the same time, we must not automatically assume that any hardship, opposition, or obstacle is an indication that we are acting according to the Lord's will. God does use practical hindrances at times to force us to recognize when we are not going in the right direction. Consider Balaam, for example, a pagan shaman who practiced sorcery and other wicked acts for profit following Israel's exodus from Egypt. He had been offered a great sum of money to cast a curse upon the Lord's people, but the Lord had warned him, "You shall not go . . . you shall not curse the people, for they are blessed" (Numbers 22:12). Nevertheless, Balaam saddled his donkey and headed out—ostensibly to bless God's people, yet in disobedience to the Lord's command just the same. As he traveled along his way on that wicked day, the Lord sent an angel to hinder his donkey's progress; He even caused the donkey to speak, showing more wisdom than his foolish master, all in order to warn Balaam that he was going the wrong way. (See Numbers 22 for the entire story.)

When we do the Lord's work, we will definitely face spiritual opposition from the enemies of God's people, and Christians must expect that. But when there's any doubt, do not assume that opposition is a "green light" on your actions; turn immediately to the Lord in prayer and meditate on His Word. The Lord never commands His people to do anything contrary to the principles of Scripture, and He might be using obstacles to open your eyes to a wrong decision.

When enemies assail you, talk to the Lord.

The Jews faced a variety of threats and opposition while rebuilding the wall. They were openly mocked and derided; they were falsely accused of evil motives and rebellious plans; they were subtly infiltrated by men who sought to discourage them and hinder their work; and they were even threatened with mass murder. But in every instance, God's people turned to the Lord in prayer and expected to find their safety and security in Him.

This is an excellent example that Christians would do well to follow. Most of us instinctively try to resolve problems by ourselves, either by trying to devise our own schemes and solutions, or by simply running away. But notice how Nehemiah responded to those who were mocking him and slandering his reputation. He did not defend himself, nor did he retaliate with sarcasm and verbal abuse. When those same enemies planned to attack the Jews violently, Nehemiah did not strike out with his own sword. In both cases, the Lord's people turned to their God in prayer.

Turning to God in prayer is not the same as abdicating responsibility, as we'll see in our next principle. One still needs to fulfill one's responsibilities, and one of those responsibilities is to use common sense while not giving in to fear and discouragement. But in the big picture, the battle belongs to the Lord, and Christians are wise to turn the fighting over to Him. Remember the words of the hymn "What a Friend We Have in Jesus" (second verse):

Have we trials and temptations? Is there trouble anywhere?
We should never be discouraged; take it to the Lord in prayer.
Can we find a friend so faithful who will all our sorrows share?
Jesus knows our every weakness; take it to the Lord in prayer.

We must be alert and prepared for battle.

Nehemiah learned of a plot to slaughter the Jews who were working to rebuild the city walls, and he didn't take that threat lightly. He knew, of course, that the true protection of God's people lay solely in God's hands, but he also understood that he had a responsibility for the safety and welfare of those under his authority. Consequently, Nehemiah took strong steps to prepare for the threat of battle. What's more, he also expected all those working on the Lord's project to remain alert and well armed. It must have been a real hindrance to the work of building, which was strenuous enough without having only one hand available, but Nehemiah felt that the work of self-defense was as important as the work of rebuilding the wall. Trust in God does not lead to inaction. Those who put their trust in the care of God also put their effort into working for His glory.

Most of us do not face the threat of physical violence for our faith (although there are many Christians in other parts of the world today who do), but this principle applies at least as much on the spiritual level. Even if our neighbors are not threatening to attack us, we all face an enemy who is even deadlier than those who opposed the Jews in Jerusalem. The devil is constantly prowling to and fro, like a fierce lion seeking someone to devour. God's people are commanded to be constantly on guard against the forces of wickedness, and we are also commanded to go everywhere well armed. Paul instructed us to carry with us "the sword of the Spirit, which is the word of God" (Ephesians 6:17). The writer of Hebrews gave further detail: "For the word of God is living and powerful, and sharper than any two-edged sword, piercing even to the division of soul and spirit, and of joints and marrow, and is a discerner of the thoughts and intents of the heart" (Hebrews 4:12).

A well-armed and vigilant Christian spends time reading and meditating daily on the Word of God. And like a well-trained soldier, a Christian also stays in close contact with his Commanding Officer through prayer and obedience. The military analogy, in fact, is very apt in life, because we live in a battle zone, where the enemy is constantly trying to destroy us. Therefore, as a believer, you must always "be sober, be vigilant; because your adversary the devil walks about like a roaring lion, seeking whom he may devour. Resist him, steadfast in the faith, knowing that the same sufferings are experienced by your brotherhood in the world" (1 Peter 5:8–9).

5. Why did Nehemiah ask the Lord to "not cover their iniquity" (v. 5)? How is this different from harboring a vindictive spirit?

6. What does it mean to resist the devil (1 Peter 5:9)? How is this done, in practical terms?

7. Why did Nehemiah make no response to the verbal abuse of the enemies? Why did he make a very practical response to their threats of violence? In what circumstances is each response most wise?

8. When have you faced opposition or problems caused by the enemy? When has the Lord used difficulties to turn you away from doing wrong? How does one tell the difference?

⤙ TAKING IT PERSONALLY ⤚

9. How do you normally respond to threats or verbal abuse? How did Jesus respond to such things? In what ways do you need to become more like Him?

10. What trials or hardships are you trying to resolve in your own strength? List them below, and spend time each day this week asking the Lord to take over the battles.

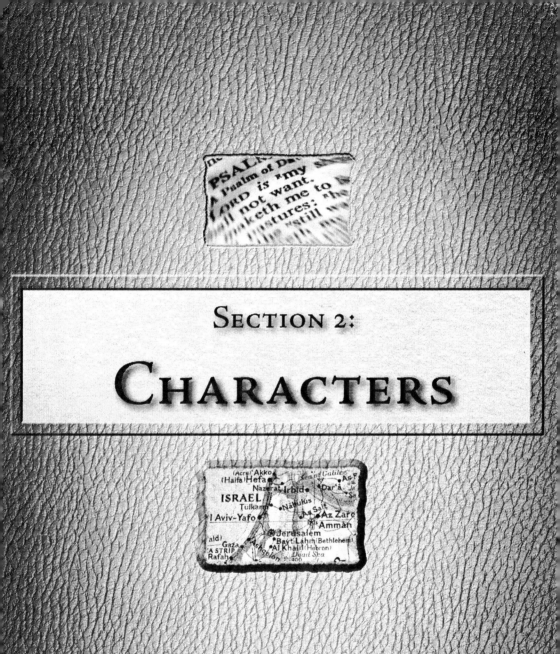

SECTION 2:

CHARACTERS

In This Section:

~ 6 ~
Ezra

↜ Character's Background ↝

Ezra was descended from a long line of priests, dating all the way back to Aaron himself, the first high priest of Israel. The Lord had appointed Aaron, Moses' brother, to take on that sacred role, and He had stipulated that only men descended from Aaron should ever follow in his steps. In this alone, Ezra would have been a good choice to lead the Jews back to Jerusalem, since they would be reestablishing the Lord's prescribed worship in the temple there.

But that was not Ezra's sole qualification. He also had spent his life studying God's Word and memorizing it—and more important, he had spent his life *obeying* it. He had become an expert in the law of God, a teacher of teachers, and a teacher by example as well as by word. The Lord had appointed him to take the lead on this important expedition because he was well qualified in obedience as well as knowledge.

As our study opens, the people are gathered and ready to leave for Jerusalem—a lengthy trip that is fraught with danger. The king issues a decree giving his blessing, and he loads the people with gold and silver to fund the work; everything is lined up and ready to go. And then Ezra discovers that some people are missing. In this study, we will discover what it means to be a follower of God who does not cut corners.

↜ Reading Ezra 7:1–28 ↝

The Lord Calls Ezra: *Ezra is a priest and a scribe, an expert in the Word of God. The Lord calls him to move to Jerusalem, and he obeys.*

1. after these things: Zerubbabel led the Jews in rebuilding the Lord's temple in Jerusalem, which was completed in 515 BC during the reign of King Darius in Persia. The events in this chapter took place many years later, under the reign of Artaxerxes, when Ezra led a second wave of Jews back to Jerusalem around 458 BC.

During the sixty-year interval between Zerubbabel and Ezra, the events of the book of Esther took place in Persia.

6. A SKILLED SCRIBE IN THE LAW OF MOSES: Ezra was descended from a long line of priests, which he traced back all the way to Aaron, the brother of Moses. He was also a scribe, one who studied and transcribed the law of Moses. This dual role made him a valuable asset to the returning Jews, who were in desperate need of instruction concerning God's Word. Tradition claims that Ezra could write out the entire law from memory.

ACCORDING TO THE HAND OF THE LORD HIS GOD UPON HIM: Once again, we are reminded that the events in all these chapters took place according to the sovereign will of God. Without God's constant intervention and protection, Jerusalem could never have been rebuilt; for that matter, the Jews themselves would have remained in exile.

7. THE PRIESTS, THE LEVITES, . . . AND THE NETHINIM: The priests were descendants of Aaron who served as the nation's spiritual leaders, overseeing the worship and sacrifices, while the Levites were members of the priestly tribe of Levi who assisted the priests. The Nethinim were descendants of the Gibeonites, who looked after the temple building, not members of the priestly class.

10. SEEK . . . DO . . . TEACH: Ezra set an ideal example of the process by which a person grows to spiritual maturity and godliness. First, he "prepared his heart" in a fixed determination to understand the Word of God, probably spending his youth in the study and meditation of the Scriptures. This process naturally fit together with immediate application, as Ezra strove to do what God's Word commanded, putting it into practice in his own life first and foremost. And this, finally, led to a natural role as a teacher of others—for one cannot teach what he has not first practiced. Ezra's life of obedience enabled him to teach God's Word; but more important, "the good hand of his God upon him" (v. 9) strengthened him and equipped him for that role.

11. EZRA THE PRIEST, THE SCRIBE, EXPERT: This is a powerful testimony to both Ezra's character and his grasp of God's Word. He had studied and memorized the Lord's commands to the point that he had become a teacher of teachers. It is also significant that he used this as his description, rather than "envoy of the king" or some other title.

THE KING'S DECREE: *King Artaxerxes writes a decree giving the Jews permission to return to Jerusalem and rebuild God's temple.*

12. ARTAXERXES, KING OF KINGS: It was true that Artaxerxes ruled over other kings, but Jesus Christ is the true King of kings and Lord of lords (cf. Revelation 19:16). Jesus alone can make that claim, since He will rule over all earthly powers in His coming kingdom (Revelation 11:15).

13. I ISSUE A DECREE: Decrees were commonly written as official documents, then reiterated in personal letters that gave an emissary authority in his travels. Ezra would have read this letter to the Jews in Jerusalem to demonstrate that he had the king's backing.

15. FREELY OFFERED TO THE GOD OF ISRAEL: It is interesting that King Artaxerxes chose to make a freewill offering to the Lord, even though he did not worship Him. He may have been hoping to appease "the god of Judah" in hopes of avoiding future trouble from that region, since people in that time thought that various gods ruled in specific geographical regions. The fact that Ezra was carrying a bounty of the king's gold and silver would make his journey to Judah that much more dangerous.

16. THE FREEWILL OFFERING OF THE PEOPLE AND THE PRIESTS: The freewill gifts of God's people were a very important part of rebuilding Jerusalem, both for the temple and the walls. We will look at this subject in Study 11.

21. THE GOD OF HEAVEN: The king's use of this phrase suggests that he had some insight into the true nature and character of God, but his repeated references to "your God" and "the God of Jerusalem" indicate that he had probably not bowed himself before the true God of all creation. Knowing who God is does not make a person a Christian; one must also submit oneself to Him as the only God, accepting His free gift of salvation. The king's question, "Why should there be wrath against the realm of the king and his sons?" (v. 23), suggests that he viewed the Lord as yet another "god" whose power was limited geographically. His gifts, therefore, were probably motivated by the hope of appeasing this unknown god of the Jews.

25. SET MAGISTRATES AND JUDGES . . . AND TEACH: The effect of this decree gave a measure of autonomy to the Jews in Judah—exactly what their enemies were striving to avoid. Yet this element of spiritual shepherding was exactly what Ezra had a heart to do. He knew that the Jews returning from captivity needed instruction in the Word of God, and that became the focus of his ministry.

27. WHO HAS PUT SUCH A THING AS THIS IN THE KING'S HEART: Once again, Ezra recognized that the king's generosity was due to the Lord's intervention. He was grateful to King Artaxerxes for his benevolence, but he also gave the final glory to God.

PREPARING FOR THE JOURNEY: *Ezra gathers the necessary people and supplies, and they prepare to make the dangerous and lengthy trip to Judah.*

15. **AHAVA:** This unknown location was near the Euphrates River in Babylon.

THE SONS OF LEVI: That is, men from the tribe of Levi. This tribe had been set apart by God to be the priestly class, and all who acted in a priestly role were descendants of Levi. The high priest was always a descendant of Aaron, a subset of the tribe of Levi, but other Levites also served in other priestly functions. Apparently, no descendant of Levi had joined Ezra for this return to Jerusalem (although others had returned previously with Zerubbabel). Ezra was deeply concerned about this situation, because he had no one qualified to serve in the temple.

17. **THEY SHOULD BRING US SERVANTS FOR THE HOUSE OF OUR GOD:** To remedy this situation, Ezra took the time and effort to find qualified men from the tribe of Levi. Others might have been tempted to look for some more expedient method, perhaps not being too concerned about meeting the Lord's qualifications for the priestly class, but Ezra was determined to obey the Lord's Word in all things— and especially on something as important as the nation's spiritual leaders.

18. **THEY BROUGHT US A MAN OF UNDERSTANDING:** Only thirty-eight Levites were willing to join Ezra in his return to Jerusalem. Many priestly tasks were repetitive and seemingly mundane, and it is quite likely that most Jews had grown comfortable in their Persian lifestyles. But the Lord raised up a remnant of men who had understanding and wisdom, and who recognized that even mundane tasks in God's service are of infinitely more value than the most glorified projects of the world. This also helps us to recognize the cost that Ezra and Nehemiah paid in leaving behind their great Persian positions to undertake the arduous task of rebuilding Jerusalem.

21. **I PROCLAIMED A FAST:** The Jews were about to leave on their four-month trek back to Judah, but before leaving they attended to the most important element of the trip: seeking God's will and protection. They wanted to be sure that the trip was His plan and not something of their own invention, and they also wanted their hearts and lives to be pure before Him.

22. **AN ESCORT OF SOLDIERS AND HORSEMEN:** As we have already seen, Nehemiah accepted his king's offer of a military escort. The trip was long and very dangerous, and the presence of the great gift of the king's gold and silver only made the caravan a more attractive target for bandits and enemies. Yet Ezra was "ashamed to request" such an escort from the king because he had previously told the king that the

Lord would protect them. He was concerned about the Lord's glory, not about their safety, and he did not want the Persians to think that his God could not live up to His promises.

26. I weighed into their hand: Once again, Ezra was carefully following the Word of God as he gave the sacred treasure into the hands of the priests (Leviticus 3). The 650 talents of silver weighed approximately twenty-five tons, and the gold weighed nearly another four tons!

28. You are holy to the Lord: The Lord had set apart the tribe of Levi to be His holy priesthood, and as such they were consecrated to His service (Numbers 3:45). In the same way, the gold, silver, and other precious objects had been set aside for the Lord's use, and in that sense they were holy in His sight.

31. the hand of our God was upon us: Once again, Ezra reminded his readers that the Lord is completely faithful to His promises and His people. The Jews had no need of a military escort, despite the fact that they were carrying a king's ransom in the caravan. The important fact for Christians to understand is that the Lord's hand is always upon His children, and He is the source of our security.

ᴄ First Impressions ᴄ

1. *According to Ezra 7:10, what three things characterized Ezra's life? How are these things done? Why are they important?*

2. *How had Ezra become an "expert" in the Word of God? What effect did that expertise have on his ministry? on the people around him?*

3. *Why did Ezra feel ashamed (8:22) to ask the king for a military escort? What motivated his decision? What does this reveal about his character?*

4. *Why did Ezra take time to find some members of the tribe of Levi before leaving for Jerusalem? What did this demonstrate about God's Word? about obedience?*

↜ Some Key Principles ↝

There are no shortcuts in obedience to God's Word.

Ezra had made many preparations for the move to Jerusalem. He had gathered a large body of Jews to join him, and each of those families had made all the necessary preparations involved in making a major, life-changing move. The king had also given Ezra his full blessing on the trip, providing him with a letter of authority to reestablish a Jewish community and rebuild the Lord's temple. He had also handed Ezra a huge sum of money and treasure, and Ezra probably felt a sense of urgency to get that money where it belonged. A host of people and plans were ready to go, only waiting for their leader to start the trip. And then Ezra discovered that there were no members of the tribe of Levi with him.

Now, human wisdom would suggest a "work-around" measure at this point. So many people were standing around, waiting to get started, and the king's money was sitting there waiting for theft—surely prudence would dictate an "ad hoc" alternate plan. But Ezra refused to begin rebuilding the temple without the leadership and assistance of God's selected priests, and he made this decision because God's Word commanded it. Ezra may have been caught by surprise, but he knew that the Lord wasn't. God wanted him to follow His prescribed methods, and He would take care of the timetable.

There are no shortcuts to obeying God's Word, and the Lord does not call His people to find "work-arounds" and "emergency interim methods." His Word gives clear guidance in our daily lives, the correct approach to worship and church structure, roles of authority and submission, and much more—much of which goes contrary to what the world believes today. When it comes to clear teachings in Scripture, there is no substitute for obedience.

The Lord calls us to seek His guidance in every undertaking.

Ezra and the Jews were ready to go. They had spent months preparing for the long journey, as well as making arrangements for a permanent change of address and lifestyle. This was no small undertaking; it was a complete change of life for everyone concerned, and it is unlikely that anyone had made the decision on the spur of the moment. Yet, when the big day had nearly arrived, Ezra stopped everything and called the people to join him in fasting and prayer to seek the Lord's guidance and blessing.

This might seem like an odd approach. This was no last-minute realization that they had forgotten to seek the Lord's guidance. The people in general and Ezra in particular had undoubtedly been in much prayer during the months of preparation. Nevertheless, when everything was prepared and the people were ready to begin, Ezra stopped to spend time before the Lord once again. Ezra had made it a habit of his life to bathe every undertaking in prayer, constantly seeking the Lord's guidance to ensure that he was going in the right direction and not overlooking anything important.

This is the pattern for all God's people, to be constantly entering His presence deliberately and without distraction. Ezra added the element of fasting in order to dedicate the prayer time fully to the Lord, blocking out all the distractions of daily life to concentrate on His voice. The person who seeks the Lord's direction for every step will never go far from His chosen path.

Study, obey, and teach.

Ezra 7:10 states that "Ezra had prepared his heart to seek the Law of the LORD, and to do it, and to teach statutes and ordinances in Israel." This statement reveals a great deal about the character of the man: he had "prepared his heart," meaning that he had consciously made it a high priority in his life, and had stuck to that priority for many years. He had sought the Lord by studying His Word, meditating on it daily and looking for ways to apply it practically in his life. He had probably also taken great pains to memorize it, as history claims that he could write the law of Moses from memory. But beyond these intellectual pursuits, Ezra had consciously applied God's Word to his life, deliberately obeying His commands on a daily basis for a long period of time.

And these habits are what equipped Ezra to become a great teacher. A person cannot hope to teach others how to play a musical instrument until he has gained some degree of mastery himself. In the same way, a person cannot teach others the Word of God unless he or she is already living by it. Not every Christian is a gifted teacher, and not all Christians are called to preach the Word from the pulpit—but every Christian *is* called to teach by example. In fact, some of the most powerful teaching is done simply by living according to God's Word, whether or not any words of explanation are ever given to those watching.

The psalmist summarized this process nicely: "How can a young man cleanse his way? By taking heed according to Your word. With my whole heart I have sought You; oh, let me not wander from Your commandments! Your word I have hidden in my heart, that I might not sin against You" (Psalm 119:9–11). The process illustrated by Ezra is threefold: study God's Word, obey God's Word, teach God's Word. This is the process all Christians are called to emulate.

ᔕ DIGGING DEEPER ᔓ

5. *If you had been in Ezra's place, what would you have done upon discovering that you had no priests with you?*

6. What "shortcuts" do some Christians take when it comes to God's Word? What is the danger of such an approach? What shortcuts have you taken in the past?

7. Why did the people take time to fast and pray before leaving on their journey? Why are the "little ones" mentioned in this context (8:21)? What effect would this have on their children?

8. Why is it so important for a Christian to spend time alone studying God's Word? What role does fasting play in this process?

9. What are you teaching to people around you each day concerning God's Word and His character? What might a casual observer learn from watching your life?

10. What decisions are you facing at present? In what ways are you submitting to God's will and casting your worries upon Him? How can you do that this week?

↜ CHARACTER'S BACKGROUND ↝

We now return to Nehemiah and his crew of faithful laborers, working diligently to rebuild the wall around Jerusalem. These people had been hard-pressed by the work, dividing their time equally between arduous physical labor and diligent security duty. At the end of a typical day, they had neither time nor energy left to attend to many of their own personal responsibilities. And those responsibilities were important, including paying their taxes and gathering enough food to feed their families.

This led many of the people into financial difficulties. They had debts that could not be paid right away, or they'd borrowed outright to pay their taxes. Some of them had to go outside the city to work as hired hands harvesting other people's crops. Many were going hungry, and they ended up being exploited by those who were more fortunate.

The Lord had given clear instructions to His people on how to be generous with the poor. But Nehemiah discovered that despite the work on the wall and the temple, the people were not obeying the laws that God had given Israel. Despite the new start in the land, many of the Jews were still reluctant to live how God commanded them to, and they began to take unfair advantage of the poor in hope of personal gain.

↜ READING NEHEMIAH 5:1–19 ↝

THE PEOPLE CRY OUT: *Work on the wall is suddenly interrupted by a great outcry from the people. They cannot pay their bills, and they are being sold into slavery.*

1. THERE WAS A GREAT OUTCRY: We now move forward in time once again to rejoin Nehemiah in his wall-building project. The people had been working very diligently, simultaneously standing guard against the threatened attack (as we saw in Study 5), and they had done so at the expense of their normal daily responsibilities.

We are told here that the outcry was from "the people and their wives," which suggests that the entire families of the workers had been affected.

AGAINST THEIR JEWISH BRETHREN: There is a sad irony here. The Jews had no complaint against the Persian government; indeed, they had reason to be very grateful to the king. The problem here was not from foreigners but from the Jews themselves, as the wealthy were taking advantage of those doing the rebuilding. These may also have been the same Jews who had refused to join the work of rebuilding, probably having formed an alliance with Sanballat and Tobias.

2. LET US GET GRAIN: There were three groups facing financial crisis. The first group had spent all their time and energy rebuilding the wall, such that they had no time left to work for their own food. These people may have been among the poorest, those who owned no property and normally would have earned a living by harvesting the fields of others.

3. WE HAVE MORTGAGED OUR LANDS: The second group were property owners who had been forced to take mortgages in order to pay their bills. There evidently was a famine at the time to make matters worse, and these people were having trouble feeding their families.

4. WE HAVE BORROWED MONEY FOR THE KING'S TAX: The third group had been hard-hit on Persian taxes, both on property and on produce. This group was the hardest hit: they had not mortgaged their lands; they had sold their children into slavery.

5. FORCING OUR SONS AND OUR DAUGHTERS TO BE SLAVES: A person who could not pay his debts might sell himself (or his son or daughter) into slavery. God's Word contains specific stipulations concerning this practice, stipulations that these wealthy Jews were not obeying. First, the Lord forbade His people to charge interest to one another on loans (Exodus 22:25). Second, the debtor was to be treated with dignity and respect as a fellow member of God's chosen people (Leviticus 25:39–40). Third, such debts might include indentured service, but it did *not* include a person's property. The Lord had given the promised land to all His people as an inheritance, and they were not permitted to buy and sell that land, even to one another (Numbers 36:7–9). Finally, even the indentured servanthood was limited to seven years, after which the entire debt was to be canceled and the servants returned to their homes and families. (There was also a special Year of Jubilee every fifty years in which all debts were automatically canceled.) Neglecting this was one of the very sins that had brought on the exile, and the Jews had already returned to it.

Nehemiah responds to this situation with great anger. But his actions in response are somewhat surprising.

6. I BECAME VERY ANGRY: Nehemiah demonstrated the difference between sinful anger and righteous indignation. His anger was kindled by the fact that the Jews were not obeying God's Word—and that was what caused them to be sent into captivity in the first place. He did not express his anger in retaliation, but addressed instead the underlying sinful behavior that was causing the problem.

7. AFTER SERIOUS THOUGHT: Nehemiah also did not "fly off the handle" in his anger, responding in the heat of the moment. He took time to reflect and seek the Lord's wisdom in how to handle it.

I REBUKED THE NOBLES AND RULERS: After praying, Nehemiah took strong action. The Hebrew phrase here implies a strong contention, even taking legal action against someone. Nehemiah did not overreact, but he did not gloss over the sin either.

8. WE HAVE REDEEMED OUR JEWISH BRETHREN: Nehemiah had, once again, set an example by his own behavior. He had personally redeemed Jews who were in servitude in Babylon, using his own money.

THEY WERE SILENCED: Nehemiah's rebuke was unanswerable, because he had founded it on two things: God's Word, and his own personal example. The fact that he had obeyed the Lord at cost to himself in this matter left no room for his opponents to argue back.

9. BECAUSE OF THE REPROACH OF THE NATIONS: Once again, Nehemiah's paramount concern was the glory of God before the rest of the world. The actions of these nobles had placed their fellow Jews in danger, but it was far worse that they had slandered God's name before their pagan neighbors.

LEADING BY EXAMPLE: *Nehemiah does more than scold the wrongdoers; he demonstrates the right way to live.*

10. I . . . AM LENDING THEM MONEY AND GRAIN: Nehemiah's actions exemplified the Lord's intentions in the law. He expected His people to lend to those in need without expectation of profit. If a person was destitute, those who had the means should give to them as a free gift. If the debtor was able to repay the money, no interest should be charged. Such generosity was a mark of true godliness (Psalm 15:1, 5).

11. RESTORE NOW TO THEM: Those who had taken advantage of their brethren were commanded to restore all the property they had confiscated, and to restore all the interest they had charged. Nehemiah called the people to obey the Lord's commands, but he did not go beyond that to mete out punishment on those who had disobeyed. Once they had restored what they had taken, the matter was closed.

14. NEITHER I NOR MY BROTHERS ATE THE GOVERNOR'S PROVISIONS: Nehemiah was entitled to collect taxes from the people in Judah because he was officially appointed as the king's representative—yet he didn't. He refrained from taxing the Jews in order to serve as an example to them of self-sacrificial love.

16. I ALSO CONTINUED THE WORK ON THIS WALL: Nehemiah dealt with issues that came up, but his central focus was always on completing the work that the Lord had called him to do. He was not there for personal profit, and did not waste his time buying land or striving to further his career. He was there to build the wall, and build he did.

17. AT MY TABLE: Nehemiah's role as governor carried certain social obligations, just as any important political official is expected to entertain influential guests today. The costs were quite high for such obligations, and previous governors had not hesitated to make the Jews pay the bill through taxes. But Nehemiah met his obligations out of his own pocket, refusing to add to the financial burden of his fellow Jews.

⌒ FIRST IMPRESSIONS ⌒

1. *What financial crisis befell the laborers in Jerusalem? What caused it? How had they become vulnerable to such a crisis?*

2. *How did God expect the nobles to respond to the needs of their brethren? Why do you think the Jewish leaders did not follow God's Law?*

3. *What made Nehemiah so angry in this situation? If you had been in his position, what would you have done?*

4. *In what ways did Nehemiah demonstrate the qualities of a strong, godly leader in this passage? What leaders have you known who were like him?*

∽ SOME KEY PRINCIPLES ∽

God is compassionate, particularly toward the poor.

Many people often assume that the Old Testament describes God as wrathful and vengeful. However, the most common word in the Old Testament used to describe God is "compassionate." God cares about people, and He particularly cares about the poor and needy who belong to Him. In this case, the poor who were being exploited were the very ones who had thrown themselves wholeheartedly into the work of rebuilding the walls, and they had stood firm through some severe persecution and opposition. They demonstrated a strong commitment to the Lord's work, and one would have expected their fellow Jews to be grateful.

Unfortunately, they were not rewarded with gratitude, but were exploited. Those who were taking advantage of them assumed that God simply would not notice or care about the exploitation of the weak. These were powerful and influential men, people with money and property, who had the capability of taking advantage of an opportunity when it arose. And they saw an opportunity for personal gain in the hardship of their fellow Jews. They did not hesitate to seize hold of it.

These men had forgotten that because He is compassionate, God hears the cry of the oppressed (Exodus 22:27). The Lord calls His people to be generous with those who are less fortunate, giving freely with no expectation of repayment. Solomon wrote, "He who has pity on the poor lends to the LORD, and He will pay back what he has given" (Proverbs 19:17). Jesus gave us practical instruction on how to do this:

> Give to everyone who asks of you. And from him who takes away your goods do not ask them back. And just as you want men to do to you, you also do to them likewise. But if you love those who love you, what credit is that to you? For even sinners love those who love them. And if you do good to those who do good to you, what credit is that to you? For even sinners do the same. And if you lend to those from whom you hope to receive back, what credit is that to you? For even sinners lend to sinners to receive as much back. But love your enemies, do good, and lend, hoping for nothing in return; and your reward will be great, and you will be sons of the Most High. For He is kind to the unthankful and evil. Therefore be merciful, just as your Father also is merciful. (Luke 6:30–36)

A godly leader leads by example.

Nehemiah was a great leader. He organized more than one trip from Persia to Judah, gathering all the materials and resources needed to undertake the mighty work of rebuilding the city walls. He also governed with wisdom, leading God's people through some very difficult circumstances. But one of the strongest elements of his leadership was his own life, as he demonstrated in three dimensions what it meant to be a godly man.

When some of the people sinned and took advantage of their brothers, Nehemiah took a firm stand, confronting the wrongdoers and leading them back into obedience. The key word there, however, is "leading." He did not *force* them into submission; he *led* them into godliness by his own example. Nehemiah did not simply tell the nobles and rulers to stop charging usury; he demonstrated the right way of giving generously and lending freely—and he set that example *before* it became a problem among the people.

A good teacher does not simply give lectures on how to master a skill; he demonstrates that mastery by performing the skill in front of his students, so that the students can learn by imitation. Jesus did this to perfection with His disciples, both teaching them and setting an example for them to imitate. This is also the prime quality of a godly leader, setting an example that his followers can imitate. The godly leader does not say, "Go forth and do it." He says, "Watch me, and do the same."

Prayer should precede action.

Nehemiah was very angry. His co-laborers had given their all for the Lord's work, sacrificing home, security, daily responsibilities, and even food in their zeal to complete the wall. And what was their reward? They were made paupers and sold into slavery because they had neglected their own needs. What's far worse, this crime had been committed by their own brethren, not by foreigners! The nobles and rulers were the very people who should have been setting an example of living by God's Word, but they were living more like the pagans around them for the sake of personal gain. If ever there was a time for righteous anger, this was it.

Yet Nehemiah's first response is a bit surprising: he gave the matter serious thought. He didn't need to think about whether or not their behavior was wrong; he needed to think about what the Lord would have him do to correct that wrong. We can be confident, based on Nehemiah's responses to other crises, that he spent ample time before the Lord on his knees, perhaps even fasting before acting. He knew that if he responded in anger, he would be following the lead of his flesh—and he wanted to follow the lead of the Holy Spirit instead.

The psalmist wrote, "The LORD is gracious and full of compassion, slow to anger and great in mercy. The LORD is good to all, and His tender mercies are over all His works" (Psalm 145:8–9). We should follow God's example. Solomon gave us some practical advice: "A soft answer turns away wrath, but a harsh word stirs up anger. The tongue of the wise uses knowledge rightly, but the mouth of fools pours forth foolishness" (Proverbs 15:1–2). "Better is a dinner of herbs where love is," wrote Solomon, "than a fatted calf with hatred. A wrathful man stirs up strife, but he who is slow to anger allays contention" (vv. 17–18). When anger arises, even righteous indignation, take time to reflect on how the Lord would have you respond, and seek Him in prayer.

↳ Digging Deeper ↲

5. Why did Nehemiah give "serious thought" (v. 7) to the situation? In practical terms, how is this done? Why is it important?

6. What were "the governor's provisions" (v. 14)? Why did Nehemiah not take advantage of what was his by right? How did this influence his rebuke of the nobles?

7. Why is God particularly compassionate to the poor among His people? Why do others often neglect them?

8. When has someone taken advantage of your misfortunes? When have you been guilty of doing that to others? What did Jesus teach on this subject?

↪ TAKING IT PERSONALLY ↩

9. When you find yourself in an emotionally charged situation, how do you usually respond? How does your normal response compare with Nehemiah's? with Christ's?

10. What leadership roles do you hold (e.g., parent, teacher, boss, group leader, etc.)? Do you tend to lead more by example or by command?

— 8 —
HAGGAI

↶ CHARACTER'S BACKGROUND ↷

Haggai was a prophet of the Lord in Jerusalem during the time of Zerubbabel. Essentially nothing is known about him apart from his own writings and the mentions made in Ezra, yet he is very specific as to the dates of his prophecies: a four-month period during 520 BC. He most likely had returned from Babylon to Jerusalem with Zerubbabel eighteen years earlier, in 538 BC, and he might even have been old enough to have been carried into captivity with Daniel in 586 BC.

The name Haggai means "festival," and at first glance this may seem ironic, given the disciplinary content of his message from God. But the Lord had sent His people to Jerusalem specifically to reinstate His prescribed worship practices and to rebuild His chosen city, and that should have been a festive occasion. If there was any loss of festivity, it was because the Lord's people had lost His perspective. They had stopped work on the temple, and instead were working to expand their own wealth. Like their ancestors who were exiled one hundred years earlier, they ceased caring about God's kingdom, and started building their own.

In this study, we will learn that the Lord wants His people to share His priorities, and we will discover what He sometimes does to get our attention. The central message of Haggai is vital to us today: consider your ways!

↶ READING HAGGAI 1:1–15 ↷

MAKING EXCUSES: *The Jews in Jerusalem have stopped building the temple, at first by compulsion but now by choice. The Lord sends His prophet with an important message.*

1. THE SECOND YEAR OF KING DARIUS: That is, August 29, 520 BC.

HAGGAI THE PROPHET: Very little is known about Haggai, apart from what he tells us in this book. He apparently traveled with Zerubbabel in the first wave of Jews to return from Persia to Judah. Joshua the high priest is called Jeshua in Ezra (Ezra 3:2).

2. The time has not come: As we saw in Study 3, the treachery of the Samaritans gained a temporary success against God's people, and the Jews had stopped working on the temple. They evidently convinced themselves that it simply wasn't God's timing to rebuild it just now, thus lulling themselves into complacency and indifference. Notice also that the Lord referred to the Jews as "this people" rather than "My people." It would be comparable to an angry man referring to "this woman" rather than "my wife."

4. time for you yourselves to dwell in your paneled houses: There is a biting irony in the Lord's words. If their own houses were falling apart, they would not casually say, "The time just hasn't come yet for us to repair the roof." The Lord's people had made their own comfort a high priority, while caring nothing about the Lord's house. They were building luxury onto their houses, while the Lord's house was in ruins.

> **Get Busy:** *The Lord commands His people to make His priorities their priorities, to stop making excuses and get started rebuilding.*

5. Consider your ways: This is the central message of Haggai's prophecies, calling upon God's people to take stock of their lives to ensure that they are living in obedience to God's Word, sharing His priorities as their own top priorities.

6. You have sown much, and bring in little: Ironically, they had stopped working on the temple to save riches for themselves, yet the Lord was disciplining them by sending drought and famine. The more they saved, the less they had. But, Haggai says, if they would make God's priorities their own, He would once again send them fullness and prosperity.

8. Go up ... and bring wood and build: Three relatively simple steps outline what the Lord required of His people in this project: Go to the forests (which had regrown during the captivity), make lumber, and start building. There was no mystery surrounding His will, and the people did not lack knowledge—what they lacked was simple obedience.

that I may take pleasure in it: The Lord's pleasure would not be from the building itself. In fact, this temple was to be a pitiful structure compared to the magnificent temple Solomon had built (2 Chronicles 2–5). The Lord would take pleasure in seeing His chosen people worshiping Him in the way He had prescribed, and His name would be glorified when the world saw them doing so.

9. I blew it away: Literally, "I sniffed at it!" The Lord snorted with contempt when He saw His people's priorities as they strove after things that could not last while ignoring the things of eternity.

EVERY ONE OF YOU RUNS TO HIS OWN HOUSE: That is, the Jews were busy running to and fro, looking after their own interests, while the house of the Lord lay in ruins. Jesus addressed this conflict of priorities: "Do not worry, saying, 'What shall we eat?' or 'What shall we drink?' or 'What shall we wear?' For after all these things the Gentiles seek. For your heavenly Father knows that you need all these things. But seek first the kingdom of God and His righteousness, and all these things shall be added to you" (Matthew 6:31–33).

11. ON ALL THE LABOR OF YOUR HANDS: The Lord did more than send drought and famine; He sent futility and frustration on all the labors of His people. He longed to bless their work with success, but first their work needed to be *His* work.

12. THE PEOPLE FEARED THE PRESENCE OF THE LORD: That is, they renewed their commitment to Him and to seeking His presence. The people's repentance came less than two weeks after Haggai began prophesying, on September 21, 520 BC.

13. I AM WITH YOU: As soon as the people repented of their false priorities and embraced God's priorities once again, He relented His hand of discipline in their lives and began to pour out His blessings. These words are among the most joyful, encouraging words of Scripture, reminding us that almighty God is always with His people in whatever situation they face.

⌁ READING HAGGAI 2:1–9 ⌁

THE LATTER TEMPLE: *The Lord sends another prophecy through Haggai, this time concerning events in the distant future, when God would build His most glorious temple.*

1. IN THE SEVENTH MONTH: October 17, 520 BC, less than a month after the people repented and renewed their work on the temple.

3. IS THIS NOT IN YOUR EYES AS NOTHING: The older Jews would have remembered the magnificence and splendor of Solomon's temple; and compared to it, this rebuilt temple must have seemed like a hovel. Yet the Lord was not discouraged, and He didn't want His people to be, because He had a far more glorious temple in the works, which no man had ever dreamed of, one not made by human hands.

4. BE STRONG: On the surface, this may sound like a platitude, akin to "cheer up." But the Lord was actually commanding His people to be strong, and strength is generally something that is not a matter of choice; a person is either physically powerful or not, according to the bodily structure with which he or she was born. Yet the strength that the Lord commands *is* a matter of choice, the choice to set one's heart on steadfast obedience regardless of the cost.

5. DO NOT FEAR: Closely related to the previous command is the command not to fear. The Israelites would have been discouraged by the small size of this temple, compared to their previous one. But God did not want them to fear the future, because He had a plan that was greater than anything they could imagine.

7. THE DESIRE OF ALL NATIONS: This refers to the Messiah, Jesus Christ. All people who have ever lived have yearned to be set free from the curse of death and to find peace with God—even if they didn't understand that this desire was at the root of all their longings. Specifically, the Lord's words refer to an event that is yet to unfold, when He would establish His kingdom on earth. In that day, all nations—indeed, the heavens and the whole earth—will be shaken (Hebrews 12:25–28; Revelation 6–9).

9. THIS LATTER TEMPLE: Haggai's audience might have thought that the temple they were building was "the latter temple," but the Lord's prophecy went far into the future. He described a future temple structure that Jesus will establish during His millennial kingdom (Ezekiel 40–48). This temple will vastly surpass any man-made structure in glory, and the nations of the earth will come to it for worship.

⌁ FIRST IMPRESSIONS ⌁

1. *Why did the Jews stop building the temple in the first place? How did that gradually grow into complacency?*

2. *God does not dwell in any physical structure or geographical region. So why was He angry that the people had not rebuilt His house? What were the larger issues involved?*

3. *How did the Lord get His message across to His people? What circumstances did He use? What people did He use? How does He do similar things today?*

4. *What does it mean to be strong, in practical terms? What does it mean to not fear? How are these things done voluntarily?*

↜ Some Key Principles ↝

It is wise to consider your ways.

The Lord sent His prophet Haggai to bring one clear message to His people: obey God even when the circumstances are difficult. The prophet proclaimed, "Consider your ways!" (Haggai 1:5). This command might be translated, "Set your mind on your way of life." In other words, it is a call for the people to consider their ultimate priorities. In effect, God proclaimed, "Make *your* priorities *My* priorities!"

This is an important discipline that God's people need to exercise on a regular basis. The priorities and perspectives of the world are *not* God's views, yet they have a way of seeping into our thinking without our even being aware of it. As Christians, we need to reassess our priorities and views daily, even moment by moment, to ensure that we are thinking the way God thinks. We do this by spending time daily studying and meditating on His Word, by seeking His wisdom through prayer, and by fellowshipping with other believers.

Paul warns his readers that this process is vital if we are to understand God's will for our lives. "I beseech you therefore, brethren, by the mercies of God, that you present your bodies a living sacrifice, holy, acceptable to God, which is your reasonable service. And do not be conformed to this world, but be transformed by the renewing of your mind, that you may prove what is that good and acceptable and perfect will of God" (Romans 12:1–2). A Christian cannot hope to understand God's perfect will unless his or her mind is constantly renewed by the Word of God. If we forget to consider our ways, we will wind up conformed to this world.

God may use obstacles and setbacks to get your attention.

The Jews living in Jerusalem had returned to God's chosen city in order to obey His commands, reestablishing His prescribed worship practices and rebuilding the temple and walls. Yet as time went along, they found themselves suffering hardship. They were faced with drought and famine, nothing seemed to prosper, and everything they undertook was met with frustration and failure. Surely this couldn't be God's will for His people who were doing His work!

And that, of course, was exactly the case. The problem was that the people were *not* doing His work; they were doing their own work and pursuing their own goals, and the Lord had sent hardship into their lives to get their attention. This is the flip side to a principle we considered in Study 5, that Christians should expect opposition when doing the Lord's work. You'll remember, however, that we added the caveat that a Christian should not ignore opposition, in case the Lord is using it to get our attention. And in this passage, we see how He sometimes does that.

This principle holds as true for us today as it did for the people in Haggai's day. When God's people refuse to share His priorities and view the world from His perspective, He will send hardship and frustration, obstacles intended to make us stop and look up. The great irony is that when the people stopped pursuing God and focused on their own needs, their own needs were not met. The more they put in their own pockets, the less they had for themselves. When Christians turn away from pursuing Christ, they get consumed by the love of the world, which can never satisfy. True satisfaction can only be found in living for Jesus, not in the riches of the world. And often, if a Christian finds himself pursuing money rather than the Messiah, the Lord will send an obstacle or a trial as a wake-up call. When that happens, we would do well to consider our ways and renew our godly perspective, for the Lord might be chastening us in order to keep us from conforming to the world.

There awaits a future glorious kingdom.

The Jews of Haggai's day were discouraged. They had returned from exile, and had labored diligently on the temple. Even when they were distracted from their task and the prophet had to rebuke them, they responded faithfully and resumed the Lord's work. Yet now, with the finished temple before them, they wept. The temple was small, and the few in the crowd old enough to remember Solomon's temple—destroyed eighty years earlier—were dismayed by the comparison. For many of the Israelites, all that was lost in the exile was finally starting to sink in.

The Lord used Haggai to encourage this beleaguered group. He pointed them to the future, to a time when a new temple would stand in Jerusalem. The very spot where they were now weeping would one day be the site of a temple the likes of which the world had never seen. It would be so glorious that the nations of the world would bring their gold and silver to Jerusalem, and the people of the world would worship there (Haggai 2:6–8). But the glory of this temple, which is also described in Ezekiel 40–48, is not found in the gold and the silver, or even in the people. Rather, Haggai said, from this temple the Lord will give peace to the world (Haggai 2:9).

We find ourselves in a similar place as the Jews in Haggai's day. The gospel has gone forth, and there are Christians around the world. Nevertheless, the world is dominated by wars and rumors of wars. Injustice is the norm, and hunger and poverty are rampant. Yet we, too, can be encouraged by the promise of God that Jesus is going to return to earth and fulfill every one of His promises. We know that He will establish His glorious kingdom on earth, and that from that temple God will return peace and order to the world.

◠ DIGGING DEEPER ◠

5. *What exactly is complacency, in your own words? What causes it? What are its results? How can a Christian guard against it?*

6. What does it mean to "consider your ways"? How is this done, in practical terms? Why is it so vital?

7. Why do people often lose sight of the Lord's priorities in their lives? How do the demands of daily life crowd out concern about the things of God? How should Christians guard against that?

8. Why were the Jews distressed at their new temple? How did Haggai encourage them? How are Haggai's words encouraging to us today?

↳ TAKING IT PERSONALLY ↰

9.   Are you facing hardship or obstacles in your life at present? Are they opposition to the Lord's work, or the Lord's attempt to get your attention?

10.   What priorities and perspectives do you share with God? Which priorities or perspectives are more like those of the world? What will you do this week to renew your mind?

～ 9 ～
ZECHARIAH

～ CHARACTER'S BACKGROUND ～

Zechariah was a priest who traveled back to Judah with the first wave of exiles, under the leadership of Zerubbabel. Tradition holds that he was also a member of the Great Synagogue, a council of 120 originated by Nehemiah and presided over by Ezra. (This council later developed into the ruling elders of the nation, called the Sanhedrin.) He is occasionally referred to as the son of his grandfather, with whom he traveled to Judah, so it is thought that his father may have died when Zechariah was young.

Zechariah was a contemporary of Haggai and began his ministry two months after Haggai gave his first prophecies. The Lord used Haggai to begin a revival, and He used Zechariah to keep it going strong. Following the time of Zechariah, prophecy from the Lord would fall silent for four hundred years—so the Lord used him to bring a rich outburst of promise for the future, to sustain the faithful remnant of His people through those silent years.

But first He asked His people to examine their hearts and motives. Fasting and sacrifice have a place, but as should be clear by this point in the study, God is far more interested in something else: obedience.

～ READING ZECHARIAH 7:1–14 ～

A QUESTION OF RELIGIOUS OBSERVANCE: *A number of Jews travel to Jerusalem to seek the Lord's will concerning their annual fasts. Now that the temple is being rebuilt, should they continue fasting?*

1. IN THE FOURTH YEAR OF KING DARIUS: Zechariah was living in Jerusalem at the same time as Haggai, and had joined Zerubbabel in the first wave of exiles returning to Judah. He gave the prophecies of this chapter in November–December 518 BC, two years before the temple was completed.

3. Should I weep: These men had journeyed from the town of Bethel to Jerusalem to ask the priests whether or not they needed to continue observing a regular schedule of fasts. The people had established a series of four annual fasts to commemorate the fall of Jerusalem, and had continued to observe those fasts throughout the captivity. But with the temple nearly rebuilt, the wailing and fasting had grown burdensome to the Jews.

God's First Response: *In the first of four responses to the question, the Lord asks the people to examine their hearts. What is their real reason for fasting?*

5. did you really fast for Me: The Lord sent a total of four responses to the question of fasting, this first one being a rebuke. The Jews, He pointed out, were not actually fasting from repentant sorrow, but only out of self-pity (Isaiah 58:3–9). There was actually only one required fast under the law of Moses, on the Day of Atonement (Leviticus 16:29).

6. do you not eat and drink for yourselves: The Lord was asking His people to truthfully examine their own hearts before Him, laying bare the true motives behind both their fasting and their eating. If their eating was for their own pleasure, the fasts were likely also driven by selfish motivations. If the people had genuinely repented of the idolatry that led them into captivity, they could stop their regimen of fasting, as the temple was being rebuilt. But if their fasting was not from true repentance, it was a waste of time in the first place.

7. Should you not have obeyed: If the people of Judah had obeyed God's Word in the first place, there would never have been any call for their self-imposed fasts. It was disobedience that brought God's discipline upon them, and He wanted them to show their repentance through obedience, not through pious religious observances.

God's Second Response: *The Lord now moves to more practical matters in His answer, calling His people to concern themselves with obedience more than with fasting.*

9. Execute true justice: The Lord here moves to His second response to the Jews' question, offering some practical examples of the obedience He desires. True justice is not influenced by a person's wealth or status, nor is it guided by any political agenda. Mercy and compassion were the opposite of what the wealthy nobles and rulers showed to those in financial crisis, as we saw in Study 7. Widows, orphans, and foreigners who lived among the Jews had no advocate to plead their cause, and were easy targets for political and financial oppression. Those who look for every opportunity to advance themselves will end up planning evil against others, hoping to maneuver themselves ahead. Repent of such things, said the Lord, and you will have no call to be fasting.

11. **BUT THEY REFUSED TO HEED:** The Lord next pointed out that the Jews' forebears had been told these exact same things—yet they had deliberately and steadfastly refused to listen. The implication of this was a warning to the present generation not to repeat the stubbornness of the previous generation, but to yield their hearts and minds in obedience to God's Word, demonstrating their godliness through loving obedience rather than outward displays of piety.

12. **THUS GREAT WRATH CAME:** The Lord was gently reminding His people that if He did not spare previous generations from stern discipline for their stubborn sinfulness, He would not spare them either if they refused to listen.

13. **I WOULD NOT LISTEN:** The previous generation had plugged their ears and hardened their hearts deliberately in order to not hear the Lord's voice, so He responded by doing the same to them. When they cried out for deliverance from captivity, He did not answer.

➤ READING ZECHARIAH 8:1–19 ➤

GOD'S THIRD RESPONSE: *The Lord now turns His eyes forward in time, and He describes a time of blessing that will extend far beyond the Jews' immediate concerns.*

2. **THUS SAYS THE LORD OF HOSTS:** This is the Lord's third response to the Jews' question concerning their fasting.

I AM ZEALOUS FOR ZION WITH GREAT ZEAL . . . I AM ZEALOUS FOR HER: This strong language, emphasizing the Lord's zeal with a triple repetition, expresses the idea that God could not bear the estrangement from His chosen people brought about by their sin. He ached and yearned to be reconciled with them and to reveal His glory among them once again.

3. **I WILL RETURN TO ZION:** This promise had many levels. Most immediately, the Lord promised that He would establish His temple once again in Jerusalem. But the day would also come in the future when God would enter Zion in the physical form of Jesus Christ. And ultimately, Christ will return to Jerusalem on a future day to establish His thousand-year kingdom on earth.

4–5. OLD MEN AND OLD WOMEN . . . BOYS AND GIRLS: The Lord had commanded His people to look after those who are weak and easily oppressed, but in the coming day there would be no enemy to threaten any of His people, as the Lord Himself will rule over the whole earth, physically present in Jerusalem.

6. IF IT IS MARVELOUS IN THE EYES OF THE REMNANT: That is, the Jews of Zechariah's day might have thought these promises sounded marvelous or hard to believe, but their lack of belief and understanding did not limit God in any way. There is nothing too hard for the Lord, and He always keeps His promises—even those that seem far-fetched (cf. Matthew 1:23).

8. THEY SHALL DWELL IN THE MIDST OF JERUSALEM: During Christ's millennial kingdom, the Jews will be regathered to Israel from all over the earth, and they will finally submit themselves to the Messianic authority of Jesus.

GOD'S FOURTH RESPONSE: *The Lord continues to expound on the countless blessings He intends for His people, enough to make them marvel. And in the end, His answer to their question is simple: Obey Me.*

9. LET YOUR HANDS BE STRONG: Here again the Lord commands His people to be resolute in their obedience. Strength of character and faith are signs of devotion to the Lord, and here that devotion was seen specifically in rebuilding His temple.

10. BEFORE THESE DAYS: This refers to the prophecies of Haggai, which we considered in the last study.

12. THE SEED SHALL BE PROSPEROUS: These promises of blessing applied in some measure to the Jews of Zechariah's day, but they also point to the future day of Christ's millennial kingdom, when God will restore the nation of Israel to full fellowship and reconciliation.

15. DO NOT FEAR: Notice how frequently this command was given in Zechariah's prophecies. Fear is the enemy of faith, causing a person to doubt that God is in control in the face of overwhelming situations. The Lord was reiterating the important truth of His absolute sovereignty over all events, as well as His unshakable commitment to show forth His blessings and faithfulness to His people. This same truth is vital for Christians of all ages, and we are commanded by God to resist fear through faith in His sovereignty.

17. ALL THESE ARE THINGS THAT I HATE: As God's people learn to share His priorities, they will grow to hate lies and evil as much as the Lord does.

19. THE FAST OF THE FOURTH MONTH: This was the Lord's fourth and ultimate answer to the Jews' original question concerning their self-appointed fasts. Turn the fasts into feasts of joy, He was saying, to rejoice over God's blessings and faithfulness. Just remember, whether in feasting or fasting, to "love truth and peace," for obedience is better than any form of religious observance.

⤳ First Impressions ⤳

1. Why had the Jews observed this cycle of fasting for so many years? What did it represent, in their view? What did it represent in God's view?

2. What is the difference between repentance of sin and sorrow over the consequences? How does a Christian distinguish between them? What is the outward result of each?

3. *Define the following in your own words, giving practical examples of each:*
True justice:

Mercy:

Compassion:

Oppression of widows or fatherless:

Oppression of foreigners or poor:

Planning evil in your heart:

4. *In what sense are religious observances a waste of time? When are they valuable? How can a Christian distinguish between these two situations?*

⌖ Some Key Principles ⌖

Obedience is better than sacrifice and fasting.

The Jews traveled to Jerusalem to seek the Lord's guidance concerning an annual series of fasts they had observed since the beginning of their captivity seventy years earlier. The fasts brought a degree of hardship upon the people, as they entailed times of mourning and self-denial, as well as abstinence from food. They were intended to represent the people's mourning over the Lord's judgment when He permitted the Babylonians to destroy Jerusalem, but now the city was being rebuilt and temple worship was being reestablished. Would the Lord object if they ended these observations?

As we have seen, the Lord was more concerned about the people's obedience than with their outward displays of religion. It is true that the Jews demonstrated a desire to obey by asking the Lord's guidance on the matter, but God probed deeper into their hearts, asking them where their deepest priorities lay. Were they truly committed to obeying His Word, or were they mostly concerned with their own comfort? Would they serve Him with whole hearts, as their predecessor David did, or would they be only halfhearted, like Solomon, and eventually wander back to foreign gods? Were they more concerned with obedience to God or with outward demonstrations of religious regulations?

The Lord addressed these questions in more detail through His prophet Isaiah. The people, He said, had performed fasts and acts of penitence on the outside, while their hearts were still wicked on the inside. The Lord wanted full obedience to His Word, not mere showmanship during occasional religious observances. "Is this not the fast that I have chosen," the Lord asked, "to loose the bonds of wickedness, to undo the heavy burdens, to let the oppressed go free, and that you break every yoke? Is it not to share your bread with the hungry, and that you bring to your house the poor who are cast out; when you see the naked, that you cover him, and not hide yourself from your own flesh?" (Isaiah 58:6–7). Samuel asked King Saul similar questions, with the same counsel: "Has the LORD as great delight in burnt offerings and sacrifices, as in obeying the voice of the LORD? Behold, to obey is better than sacrifice, and to heed than the fat of rams" (1 Samuel 15:22). Obedience to God's Word is the only sacrifice the Lord wants from His people.

The Lord yearns for your fellowship.

The Lord told His people, "I am zealous for Zion with great zeal; with great fervor I am zealous for her" (Zechariah 8:2). Many modern Bibles translate "fervor" as "wrath," which captures the burning passion the Lord was expressing. "I burn for you with a jealous fire," the Lord was effectively saying, "a zealous and jealous love that will tolerate no competition." The Lord yearned so deeply for the love and fellowship of His chosen people that it was like a consuming fire, destroying anyone or anything that prevented their full reconciliation.

It is interesting that the Lord referred to the zeal of His love in this context. The Jews had been very zealous themselves in maintaining a cycle of fasts over a period of seventy years during their captivity. "Should I weep in the fifth month and fast as I have done for so many years?" they asked (Zechariah 7:3), implying that they had not permitted anything to prevent them from this religious observance. But the Lord called them to search their hearts and question what they were truly fasting for. Were they mourning the loss of God's close fellowship, which they had once enjoyed as His chosen nation, or were they mourning over their own suffering and misfortune? The two are not the same!

The Lord wanted His people to be zealous in seeking His face and entering His holy presence. Now, this might well be associated with certain spiritual activities, such as commemorating the Lord's Supper, as Jesus commanded (Luke 22), but those activities themselves are hollow and meaningless if one's heart is not fully committed to living in fellowship with God. The Lord has a burning zeal for your fellowship, for your company, and He wants you to share that same zeal for Him.

Jesus is coming again, and the day may be very soon.

The Lord's prophecies of blessing in these chapters had some immediate application to the Jews of Zechariah's day, but they also looked forward to future events. For example, His promise to return to Zion (Zechariah 8:3) indicated that He would rebuild His temple in Jerusalem during their day, yet it also looked ahead to the wonderful day when He would enter Jerusalem in physical form through His Son, Jesus Christ. And the promise has yet another level of fulfillment still to come, when Jesus returns to earth to establish His thousand-year earthly kingdom centered in Zion.

Scripture is clear on this final fulfillment, that Jesus is coming again—but this time not as a helpless babe lying in a manger. He will return in His strength and glory, and He will establish a kingdom that rules all the nations of the earth with a "rod of iron" (Psalm 2:9; Revelation 2:27; 19:15). In that day, the nation of Israel shall once again be the seat of blessing to all peoples (Zechariah 8:13), while the enemies of God and of His people shall be broken without remedy.

We live in the age of grace, when God's gift of salvation is readily available to anyone through faith in the gospel. But the day of grace will not last forever; the day is coming when the Lord "will gather out of His kingdom all things that offend, and those who practice lawlessness, and will cast them into the furnace of fire. There will be wailing and gnashing of teeth" (Matthew 13:41–42). The day of Christ's return is drawing close; to the Christian this means to "look up and lift up your heads, because your redemption draws near" (Luke 21:28). But for those who have not received salvation and eternal life through Jesus Christ, the Lord calls out, "Behold, now is the accepted time; behold, now is the day of salvation" (2 Corinthians 6:2).

ᴐ Digging Deeper ᴐ

5. What things does God hate? Why does He hate them? How does your own list of "hates" compare with God's list?

6. The Jews asked a fairly straightforward question, but the Lord's answer was lengthy and complex. Why? What deeper truth was He trying to dig out?

7. What did God mean when He said, "I was jealous for Zion with great jealousy, and I was jealous for her with great fury" (Zechariah 8:2 KJV)? How does His zeal for your fellowship compare with yours for His?

8. *What signs are there that Jesus' return is imminent? How does this affect your daily life? How might your priorities change in the coming week?*

⌁ Taking It Personally ⌁

9. *Does your daily life reflect true obedience to God's Word, or do you tend to "go through the motions" of religious observances? What area of obedience might the Lord be calling you to this week?*

10. *Have you received God's gift of salvation through Jesus Christ? If not, what is preventing you from doing so right now?*

Section 3:

Themes

In This Section:

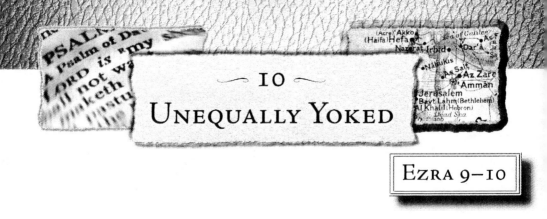

UNEQUALLY YOKED

↪ THEMATIC BACKGROUND ↩

We return once again to Ezra and his fellow Jews as they return to Jerusalem. They have not been there long—probably around four months—and Ezra has finally gotten everything in order. He had a lot of details to attend to, disseminating the money and treasure the king had given him, appointing spiritual leaders, leading the people in worship to the Lord, and all the myriad details of establishing a new home for himself and many others. Now that those details are completed, however, it should be time to buckle down and get busy with the project of rebuilding the temple.

Or so one would think. Unfortunately, no sooner had Ezra gotten things in order than he was confronted with an unexpected problem: many of the Jews had married foreign spouses! This must have seemed incomprehensible to Ezra, since that was the very sin that had led the nation of Israel into captivity in the first place. But human nature is always prone to wander from the will of God. As Solomon wrote, "As a dog returns to his own vomit, so a fool repeats his folly" (Proverbs 26:11).

In this lesson, we will see marriage from God's perspective, and we will discover that He takes it very seriously. But more importantly, we will see that while the Jews may have gotten a new start, they were still in need of the new covenant and the Messiah to change their hearts.

↪ READING EZRA 9:1–15 ↩

RETURNING TO FORMER SINS: *Ezra has just recently arrived in Jerusalem with a group of returning exiles, and almost immediately the people fall into old patterns of sin.*

1. **WHEN THESE THINGS WERE DONE:** Ezra had just brought a large group of returning exiles to Jerusalem, and they had not been there very long when the following events transpired.

HAVE NOT SEPARATED THEMSELVES: When the Israelites were on their way to the promised land, the Lord had commanded them to keep themselves apart from the people of Canaan when they arrived. In fact, He had even ordered them to make war against many of the pagan nations, destroying their altars and religious sites that were dedicated to false gods. If they failed to do this, the Lord warned, they would wind up becoming just like their pagan neighbors, intermarrying and adopting their idolatrous ways (Exodus 34:10–16; Deuteronomy 7:1–6). Unfortunately, the Israelites had not obeyed the Lord's commands in this regard, and it was the resulting intermarriages and idolatry that caused the Lord to send them into captivity in the first place. It was a sad statement on the human condition to find the returning Jews immediately beginning to repeat their former sins. It is compounded by the fact that the priests and Levites—the nation's spiritual leaders—had joined in.

2. TAKEN SOME OF THEIR DAUGHTERS AS WIVES FOR THEMSELVES: Malachi added that some of these people even divorced their Jewish wives in order to marry foreigners (2:14–16).

THE HOLY SEED IS MIXED WITH THE PEOPLES OF THOSE LANDS: This is a powerful expression that can help us understand why God does not want His people to intermarry with unbelievers. The Lord had chosen Abraham and his descendants to be the race into which He would bring the Messiah, His holy and sinless Son, Jesus. As such, the Lord wanted Abraham's descendants to be set apart as a holy people, distinct from the world around them, rather than blending in. This same principle applies to God's people today, for the Christian church is the bride of Christ, and the Lord demands that His bride keep herself apart from the world.

THE HAND OF THE LEADERS AND RULERS HAS BEEN FOREMOST: It was bad enough that the people of Judah had fallen immediately back into their former sins, but it was unconscionable and inexcusable that the spiritual leaders were actually leading the way. When the leaders go in the wrong direction, the rest of the people can only be expected to follow.

EZRA GRIEVES: *Ezra's immediate response is to fall before the Lord in deep mourning. Yet, as God's chosen leader, he identifies himself with the people of God.*

3. TORE . . . PLUCKED . . . SAT DOWN: Ezra's response was a threefold display of the tremendous grief he felt when he learned of the people's sin. He knew that their wanton disregard of God's Word would lead to sorrow, on both the personal and national levels—for the sin that brought God's discipline in the past could only bring it again in the future.

98

4. EVERYONE WHO TREMBLED: There were still some in Judah, including Ezra, who took the Lord's Word very seriously. They undoubtedly gathered together to intercede for the nation, yet their action of gathering with Ezra also made a public statement that they were not joining together with those who were in sin. If God's people refuse to separate themselves from the world, then those who still fear God's Word will separate themselves from them.

6. OUR INIQUITIES . . . OUR HEADS . . . OUR GUILT: Notice how Ezra identified himself with the people who were in sin, even though he had not participated in that sin. He recognized that sin is like leaven: a little bit of it can infect the entire nation. But he was also demonstrating an important element of spiritual leadership, identifying himself with the entire body of God's people and remembering that he, too, was a sinner.

7. WE HAVE BEEN VERY GUILTY: Ezra also understood that God takes sin very seriously, and that included the sins of intermarriage and divorce.

8. A PEG IN HIS HOLY PLACE: That is, the remnant of God's people in Judah have been firmly fixed in God's holy place, as a peg is firmly fixed in a wall.

⤳ READING EZRA 10:1–19 ⤳

PUTTING AWAY THE WIVES: *Ezra's solution to the problem is to call upon the people to put away any unbelieving spouses. It is imperative that God's people be separate from the world.*

1. THE PEOPLE WEPT VERY BITTERLY: When confronted with their sin, the people of Judah did exactly the right thing: they repented and mourned over their wickedness. This is what God desires to see when His people commit sin (and we all are sinners). He wants us to turn away from the sinful behavior, confess that we have committed sin, and be forgiven (1 John 1:9).

3. TO PUT AWAY ALL THESE WIVES: Ezra commanded the people to divorce any unbelieving wives, sending them back to their pagan families along with any children they had borne to their Jewish husbands. We must remember, however, that Ezra is a book of history, recording actual historical events. The fact that a person did something in Israel's history does not mean that it is a model of God's ideal plan for us to follow. God hates divorce (Malachi 2:16).

6. HE ATE NO BREAD AND DRANK NO WATER: This was an unusually stringent fast; people generally only fasted from food, not from water. It indicated the depth of

Ezra's grief and consternation over this situation, which underscores the seriousness of marrying an unbeliever.

8. HE HIMSELF WOULD BE SEPARATED FROM THE ASSEMBLY: The people of Judah needed to separate themselves from anyone who had married an unbeliever, lest the unbeliever in their midst lead others into idolatry.

17. THEY FINISHED QUESTIONING ALL THE MEN: This verse indicates that Ezra and the other spiritual leaders considered each case individually, and it is likely that each foreign wife was given the opportunity to openly forsake her former false gods and embrace the only true God. Such repentance would change the marriage from an unequal yoking to a proper marriage between believers. The list of those who divorced their pagan wives seems rather short, considering the frequent references to "many of us" (e.g., v. 13), so it is possible that at least some of the unbelieving spouses repented of their pagan ways and embraced God's truth.

∽ FIRST IMPRESSIONS ∽

1. *Why did Ezra respond so vehemently to the Jews' marrying foreigners? Why was that such a big problem for God's people?*

2. *Why had the Jews married foreigners in the first place? Consider the circumstances they were experiencing, having moved to a new home far from Persia. What factors might have made such marriages seem acceptable at the time?*

3.   Why does God condemn intermarriage? What dangers does it pose to a believer? to the children? to the church as a whole?

4.   How do some Christians justify marriage to unbelievers as "no big deal"? What arguments do they use? What does God's Word say on the matter?

⁀ SOME KEY PRINCIPLES ⁀

God hates divorce.

Ezra's solution to the dire problem of intermarriage in Jerusalem was to call upon the people to divorce their unbelieving spouses. His reason for such an extreme approach was that the sin itself was very extreme. As we have already considered, it was intermarriage with Israel's pagan neighbors that led God's people into the deadly sin of idolatry in the first place. Desperate circumstances sometimes call for desperate measures, and this solution may well have been the best.

Yet we must also understand that divorce is *not* God's desire for His people. Indeed, God uses very strong language on the subject. "'Take heed to your spirit, and let none deal treacherously with the wife of his youth. For the LORD God of Israel says that He hates divorce, for it covers one's garment with violence,' says the LORD of hosts. 'Therefore take heed to your spirit, that you do not deal treacherously'" (Malachi 2:15–16). Notice the words that the Lord used to describe divorce: *treachery* and *violence*. This is because when a Christian divorces his spouse, he is treacherously betraying the vows he made before the Lord, and he is violently tearing asunder a couple who are one flesh.

Jesus expounded further on this subject. "Have you not read that He who made them at the beginning 'made them male and female,' and said, 'For this reason a man shall leave his father and mother and be joined to his wife, and the two shall become one flesh'? So then, they are no longer two but one flesh. Therefore what God has joined together, let not man separate" (Matthew 19:4–6). The Jews who were listening to Jesus then asked Him why Moses had permitted divorce, and Jesus answered, "Moses, because of the hardness of your hearts, permitted you to divorce your wives, but from the beginning it was not so. And I say to you, whoever divorces his wife, except for sexual immorality, and marries another, commits adultery; and whoever marries her who is divorced commits adultery" (vv. 8–9). Jesus did make an exception in the case of an adulterous spouse, who has already been treacherous and violent toward the sacred union. As a general rule for believers, however, divorce is not God's plan.

Christians should not marry unbelievers.

To the modern reader, Ezra's reaction to the Jews marrying foreign women might seem extreme, but we must take care not to thrust modern sensibilities onto the text of God's Word. Ezra's response to the situation demonstrated how seriously the Lord takes the sin of intermarriage. Indeed, the fact that the Jews were returning from captivity and spending their time rebuilding the temple and walls indicates that God does indeed take intermarriage very seriously—for it was that very sin that led the nation of Israel into idolatry in the first place, causing them to be sent away and their city destroyed.

The Bible refers to Christians who are married to non-Christian as being "unequally yoked." The word picture is drawn from a pair of oxen that a farmer would use to pull his plow, the two animals connected with a firm collar, or yoke. If the two oxen have different ideas concerning their roles as plow pullers, they will pull the plow in different directions, one trying to go left, and the other pulling toward the right. The result to the farmer and his plow is self-evident: the work would come to a standstill, and the plow itself might be destroyed in the contest of wills.

Scripture makes it very clear that a Christian has no business marrying a non-Christian. Paul warned us clearly, "Do not be unequally yoked together with unbelievers. For what fellowship has righteousness with lawlessness? And what communion has light with darkness?" (2 Corinthians 6:14–15).

But what about a Christian who is already married to an unbeliever? The New Testament gives two principles: First, the Christian should remain in the marriage. He or she is not permitted to seek a divorce even though the marriage is unequal, because God hates divorce. Paul gave this direction in 1 Corinthians: "If any brother has a wife who does not believe, and she is willing to live with him, let him not divorce her. And a woman who has a husband who does not believe, if he is willing to live with her, let her not divorce him" (7:12–13).

But Paul also gave a second principle: if an unbeliever is married to a Christian, and the unbeliever wants a divorce, the Christian should let the unbeliever go. Paul wrote, "If the unbeliever departs, let him depart; a brother or a sister is not under bondage in such cases. But God has called us to peace" (v. 15). A Christian who is unequally yoked is in a difficult situation. But if the unbeliever wants out of the marriage, the Christian is called to live in peace, and trust the Lord through the situation.

A new start is not a new heart.

The Jews returned to the land with such promise. Their idols had been put away, and only those who wanted to work on the temple returned to the land. This was a new beginning for Israel, and the sins of the previous generations of Jews must have been a distant memory. Yet as soon as they were in the land they were imitating their parent's sins. Ezra found them marrying foreign women, Haggai found them loving money rather than God, and Nehemiah found them exploiting the poor. It was as if the exile had never happened!

The main lesson of these books (Ezra, Nehemiah, Haggai, and Zechariah) is that apart from the new covenant, true obedience to God's Word is impossible. The Israelite history bears testimony to this fact. God repeatedly started over and the Israelites repeatedly failed. He started over with Noah and his family, and sin gripped them immediately off the ark. He started over with Moses and a new nation, and ended up killing every one of them (except Joshua and Moses) in the wilderness. Now God had purified Israel and removed their entire nation, but they were back into their sinful ways again.

This illustrates that a new start does not necessarily indicate a new heart. This is the lesson that Jesus gave Nicodemus, who was a leader of the Jews. Jesus told him that unless a person is born again, he cannot even see the kingdom of God (John 3:3). Nicodemus thought Jesus was telling him to start his life over, and wondered how that was even possible. But Jesus told him that without a new heart, fresh starts would simply produce fresh failures. The Jews were learning the lesson that they did not need their land, their temple, or their wall; they needed their Messiah.

⤳ DIGGING DEEPER ⤶

5. *Why does God hate divorce? Why did Jesus make an exception in the case of adultery? How are adultery and divorce similar?*

6. *What does it mean to be "unequally yoked"? What can you learn about intermarriage from the "ox and plow" metaphor? How does this principle apply in other areas of life besides marriage?*

7. *Why did Paul counsel believers not to divorce an unbelieving spouse? What did he mean when he said, "God has called us to peace" (1 Corinthians 7:15)? How is peace an important issue in an unequal marriage?*

8. Why did the Jews fall back into sin again when they returned to the land? What does this teach us about the human heart? What is the solution for their sin?

⤙ TAKING IT PERSONALLY ⤚

9. How do these passages affect your own views of marriage? of divorce? of singleness? How do these teachings apply in your own life?

10. How does living with a new nature affect your struggle with sin? Do you find yourself like the Israelites, trapped in sin? Or do you experience the freedom that comes with a relationship with Jesus?

~ II ~
WORSHIPING GOD

↜ HISTORICAL BACKGROUND ↝

The wall has finally been completed, and the people of Judah have settled into their homes in God's chosen city of Jerusalem. The people gathered together in Jerusalem in the seventh month (September–October 445 BC), less than a week after finishing the walls, to observe the Feast of Tabernacles (Leviticus 23:33–44). And at the end of that feast, the people gathered once more to worship God as a reunited nation, humbling themselves and acknowledging their dependence on Him.

The focal point of this section is not walls, not the enemies of God, not a great leader, not even the people of God. The focal point is God Himself. The public reading of the Word of God (seen in Nehemiah 8) has pricked the hearts of the weary wall-builders. The result is that the listeners have been reminded of God's greatness and of their own failure to adequately live for His glory. This section will require some self-examination, and that can be a humbling and painful experience. Yet if we are to fully understand God's grace and mercy, we must also understand our own condition as sinners; and if we are to praise Him for His love and mercy, we must also remind ourselves of all He has done on our behalf.

This chapter consists largely of an extended prayer of praise and worship, led by the Levites before the reconstituted nation of Israel. (For further information on specific details, see the previous books in this series.) This study is designed to lead you and others to worship God.

↜ READING NEHEMIAH 9:1–38 ↝

THE PEOPLE PREPARE FOR WORSHIP: *The Jews assemble in Jerusalem for a time of national worship and repentance. Before they begin, however, they prepare themselves.*

1. ON THE TWENTY-FOURTH DAY OF THIS MONTH: We now jump to 445 BC, thirteen years after Ezra's confrontation of the people for marrying pagan spouses (Study 10).

WITH FASTING, IN SACKCLOTH, AND WITH DUST ON THEIR HEADS: These were outward demonstrations of deep mourning and sadness for their sins. Their actions seem to have been performed in the spirit of the Day of Atonement, which was observed on the tenth day of this same month.

2. SEPARATED THEMSELVES FROM ALL FOREIGNERS: This call for divorcing all lawful wives taken from among the heathen was needed, since the last time, prompted thirteen years before by Ezra, had been only partially successful. Many had escaped the required action of divorce and kept their pagan wives. Perhaps new defaulters had appeared also, and were confronted for the first time with this necessary action of divorce. Nehemiah's efforts were successful in removing this evil mixture.

3. READ FROM THE BOOK OF THE LAW . . . CONFESSED AND WORSHIPED: God's Word is the foundation of the worship process. Its truths confront the sin in our lives, and at the same time they reveal the character of God. Apart from His Word, there is no way to know Him, and so the rest of this prayer is built on the foundation of the study of the Word.

5. STAND UP AND BLESS THE LORD: The Levites led Israel in a corporate outpouring of confession and worship. They rehearsed the nation's history, beginning before creation, moving through the call of Abraham, and working their way to the present, confessing their repeated stubbornness and sins while also recognizing God's patience and goodness. It was a time of national humility and public confession, set against the backdrop of God's great mercy and forgiveness. The end result of the three-hour worship service was a national promise of obedience to God in the future (v. 38).

BEFORE THE BEGINNING: *The Levites lead the people in worship chronologically through the history of Israel. They begin at the best place—before the beginning.*

---

6. YOU ALONE ARE THE LORD: The worship service began with a fundamental truth: there is only one God, and He alone rules all things in heaven and on earth. It was important for the people to begin with this foundational understanding, since they had been yielding already to the temptation to embrace the beliefs of the world, which included a vast pantheon of make-believe gods. The Levites also were leading the people through a chronological remembrance of who God is and what He had done for them, so it was appropriate that they begin before the world was even created, when God alone existed.

YOU HAVE MADE HEAVEN: This was a summary of God's creation, which encompasses not merely heaven and earth, but absolutely all that exists. God created everything, and He did so in six twenty-four-hour days. Evolution is not a new lie, and ancient cultures had their own versions of it. The Jews were reminding themselves that the world's teachings are utterly false concerning the origins of man. (See book 1 in this series, *Before Abraham*, for more information.)

7. **WHO CHOSE ABRAM**: God called Abram; Abram did not seek out God. He chose Abram simply because He chose to set His love upon him, and He had been faithful ever since to the promises He made. See Genesis 12 and 17.

8. **YOU FOUND HIS HEART FAITHFUL BEFORE YOU**: Abraham had demonstrated a determination to obey the Lord's commands, most aptly illustrated in his willingness to sacrifice his only son at God's request (Genesis 22). Unfortunately, Abraham's descendants did not exhibit the same level of faithfulness to God's Word.

YOU HAVE PERFORMED YOUR WORDS: One of the themes of this song of praise is that God always keeps His promises, and He alone is righteous.

THE EXODUS: *The prayer now moves forward in time to the period when the Israelites were slaves in Egypt, following them on their exodus to the promised land.*

9. **OUR FATHERS IN EGYPT**: Verses 9–12 consider the events surrounding Israel's exodus from Egypt.

10. **SIGNS AND WONDERS AGAINST PHARAOH**: The Lord had sent a series of ten plagues upon the people of Egypt for their hardness of heart in refusing to allow His people to leave. The final plague was the death of every firstborn son in every household within Egypt, except those that were covered by the blood of a lamb on the doorposts. This event led to the annual celebration of Passover, and it also pictured the eventual sacrifice for sin offered by Christ on the cross.

11. **YOU DIVIDED THE SEA BEFORE THEM**: The Lord allowed His people to encounter an immovable obstacle—the Red Sea—while seeing their enemies hard on their heels behind. He then miraculously parted the sea before them, allowing them to walk across on dry ground, and slammed the sea shut on the heads of those same powerful enemies (Exodus 14). God sometimes leads us through difficult circumstances in order to demonstrate His omnipotent sovereignty.

12. **CLOUDY PILLAR ... PILLAR OF FIRE**: The Lord made His presence known to the people of Israel night and day on their exodus from Egypt. During the day, He provided an immense cloud covering, which shielded them from the hot desert sun, and by night He provided some sort of flaming element in the sky above, which allowed them to see in the utter darkness. These miraculous displays served the Israelites, but they also made known God's presence to the world around.

13. JUST ORDINANCES AND TRUE LAWS: The Lord also came among His people during their journey and taught them how to live according to His plan. The Law given to Moses was designed to make the Jews noticeably different from the rest of the world, so that other nations would see the goodness and uniqueness of Israel's God.

15. BREAD FROM HEAVEN . . . WATER OUT OF THE ROCK: Both the manna from heaven (Exodus 16) and the water from the rock (Exodus 17) miraculously provided for the Israelites' physical needs in a dry and barren land. But they also provided small pictures of God's ultimate plan of salvation through His Son Jesus, who is the "bread of life" (John 6:35).

A MISERABLE CONTRAST: *The Levites now turn their attention from God's character to their own, considering the behavior of their forefathers and themselves.*

16. THEY AND OUR FATHERS ACTED PROUDLY: The Levites turned their consideration from the character of God to themselves and their ancestors—and the comparison is not pretty. Interestingly, they used the same phrase "acted proudly" to describe Pharaoh and the Egyptians (v. 10), implying that God's chosen people had proved no different from the world. They hardened their necks just as Pharaoh had hardened his heart, stubbornly refusing to obey God's commands.

17. THEY WERE NOT MINDFUL OF YOUR WONDERS: The Lord had performed countless dramatic miracles to demonstrate His power and presence, yet the people had ignored them. It was not even that they were not paying attention and didn't notice, but that they had deliberately refused to acknowledge His faithfulness. They had made themselves blind by choice.

BUT YOU ARE GOD: Two of the most joyful words in Scripture are "but God." The Israelites had deliberately hardened their hearts, but God remained faithful. They had sinned in every way, but God remained ready to pardon. They had wandered away from Him repeatedly, but God did not forsake them. The entire human race deserves God's wrath, but God provides the free gift of salvation.

18. THEY MADE A MOLDED CALF FOR THEMSELVES: The human heart is constantly seeking to make gods from the material world—the world that was created by the only true God. This trend has not changed in modern times. (See Exodus 32 for the account of the golden calf.)

WILDERNESS WANDERINGS: *Next the Levites' prayer addresses the forty years spent wandering in the wilderness on the way to the promised land.*

19. IN THE WILDERNESS: Verses 19–21 address the wilderness period, when Israel wandered the desert under God's hand of discipline (Numbers 9–21).

20. YOUR GOOD SPIRIT TO INSTRUCT THEM: Christians can say this with an even greater significance, as God sends His Holy Spirit to reside in the life of every believer (John 14:26).

21. THEY LACKED NOTHING: Even during an extended time of discipline for stubborn sin, the Lord still met their every need. They wandered in the wilderness for forty years, but their clothes and shoes never wore out!

POSSESSION TO PRESENT: *The Levites' prayer moves through the time when Israel took possession of the promised land, up to the present moment in Judah.*

22. YOU GAVE THEM KINGDOMS AND NATIONS: Verses 22–25 address the period of taking possession of the promised land (Numbers 20–Joshua 24).

26. NEVERTHELESS: If "but God" are two joyful words in Scripture, here we find a very sorrowful one. The Lord had poured out blessing after blessing upon His people, demonstrating His power, sovereignty, faithfulness, and love. Nevertheless, the people remained rebellious and disobedient. Human nature is no different today. Verses 26–31 describe the period of the judges all the way through to the captivity; verses 32 and following address their present situation.

33. YOU ARE JUST IN ALL THAT HAS BEFALLEN US: The people asked the Lord to help them in their present distresses, yet they still recognized that those distresses had befallen them because of their own sins. They did not blame God, but they also did not refrain from asking for His mercy and help.

⌁ FIRST IMPRESSIONS ⌁

1. *What preparations did the people make before spending time in worship? What did these things mean? Why were they important? What parallels might they have in your life?*

2. *Why did the Levites work chronologically through the history of Israel in their worship? How might this help a person recognize both God's goodness and man's sin?*

3. *Why did the worship begin with God's preexistence and role as Creator of the universe? In what sense are these truths fundamental to an accurate understanding of His character?*

4. *What miraculous provisions did God make for His people throughout Israel's history? What miraculous provisions has He made in your life?*

⤚ Some Key Principles ⤙

God is the Creator and Sustainer of the universe.

Before anything existed, God was. He is beyond and apart from everything, self-sustaining and self-sufficient. Even His name "I Am" suggests this (Exodus 3:14). God created all things that exist in just six days, creating everything out of nothing with the mere power of His Word: "God said . . . and there was" (Genesis 1:3). He called the stars into existence and fixed them in place; He created the sun and moon to give light to the earth; He created the earth and the heavens to manifest the glory of His character.

But God did not create the universe and then walk away to do something else. He continues to maintain His creation, taking an abiding interest in and demonstrating love for everything He made—especially people. This is what the Levites had in mind when they said to God, "You preserve them all" (Nehemiah 9:6). God preserves and sustains His entire creation, controlling all events in a constant unfolding of His perfect plan through His absolute sovereignty—a plan that He had in mind before the beginning, before the creation of the universe.

God is both eternal and immutable. He has always existed, with no beginning and no ending, yet He has not changed in any way since before creation. He is the same yesterday, today, and forever (Hebrews 13:8). His plan to bring salvation to all people has been unfolding since before the beginning, and His plan to complete His work of salvation will continue through the end of the ages. This is one of the many reasons we join the Levites in finding God worthy of worship and praise!

God is gracious, even with the presumptuous.

The constant theme of the Levite's praise was the graciousness of God. In fact, the entire prayer is a litany of God's acts of compassion toward His people. Ever since the first sin plunged all of humanity into sin, God has been graciously working to bring peace and reconciliation to the earth. Immediately after Adam sinned, God told the serpent that from Eve's "seed" would come a Man who would crush Satan (Genesis 3:14). From that point forward, history—much of which is recounted by the Levites in our chapter here—has been leading up to that Person.

In the meantime, though, the world continued to rebel, and God continued to respond to each rebellion with a mixture of punishment, discipline, and graciousness. He destroyed the world, yet started over with one family. He scattered the nations when He shattered the Tower of Babel, but He then chose one new nation, from whom He would bless all the families of the earth (Genesis 12:3). And when that new nation, Israel, rebelled against Him in the wilderness, God disciplined them, but also graciously guided them through their wanderings by a cloud and supernatural light.

God was faithful and gracious to His people Israel during Moses' day, and He is still faithful and gracious to His people today. The difference is that now, God has sent His Son in the ultimate act of His graciousness. Jesus came as a sacrifice for sin, and in the consummate act of kindness, He gave His life for people who hated Him and wanted Him dead. As a result, the news of the gospel is really the news that God's graciousness has conquered the hearts of the presumptuous sinners. Jesus' grace is stronger than the hardest of sinner's hearts.

Praise God for His attributes.

Meditate on some of God's attributes; then spend time in prayer, thanking God for who He is.

Omnipotence: He is all-powerful, "able even to subdue all things to Himself" (Philippians 3:21).

Omniscience: God knows all things, and there is nothing hidden from Him (Revelation 2:23).

Alpha and Omega, Beginning and End: God described Himself as "I AM WHO I AM" (Exodus 3:14; Revelation 1:8). He sustains all things in the universe He created, and without Him nothing could exist.

Ready to pardon: Jesus demonstrated this quality at the very point of His death, calling upon the Father to forgive the ones who crucified Him (Luke 23:34).

Gracious and merciful: He pours out mercy and tenderness on His creation, even when we deserve His judgment (Hebrews 2:17).

Slow to anger: God's people through the ages have frequently put His grace to the test, persisting in stubborn sin despite His goodness—yet He has held back His hand of judgment (Psalm 103:8).

Keeps covenant and mercy: The Levites recognized this attribute of God's character as they worked their way through the history of Israel. The Lord's people frequently violated their covenant with God, but God never failed to keep it and to show mercy on His people (Nehemiah 9:32).

✑ DIGGING DEEPER ✑

5. In what ways did Israel betray God throughout its history? Why did God continually forgive and restore the people? What does this reveal about God? about human nature?

6. Consider God's triune nature: Father, Son, and Holy Spirit. How is each person unique? How are all three perfectly united? How might these truths influence your worship?

7. Why is worship important to individual Christians? to the church as a whole? What is involved in worshiping the Lord?

8. Review the list of God's attributes in the third principle, putting each into your own words. Add other attributes of His nature to the list, with Scripture references.

⌁ TAKING IT PERSONALLY ⌁

9. Spend time in self-reflection and confession, acknowledging sin and shortcomings and failures.

10. How do you see God's graciousness triumphing over sin in your own life?

TIMETABLE OF EVENTS

EVENT	DATE*	STUDY NUMBER
Judah carried to Babylon	586	—
Zerubbabel returns with first wave	538	1
Temple rebuilt	515	8
Haggai and Zechariah begin to prophesy	520	8, 9
Events of Esther	486–465	—
Ezra returns with second wave	458	2, 3, 6, 10
Nehemiah returns with third wave	444	4, 5, 7, 11

* All dates are BC. Dates are approximate.

Notes and Prayer Requests

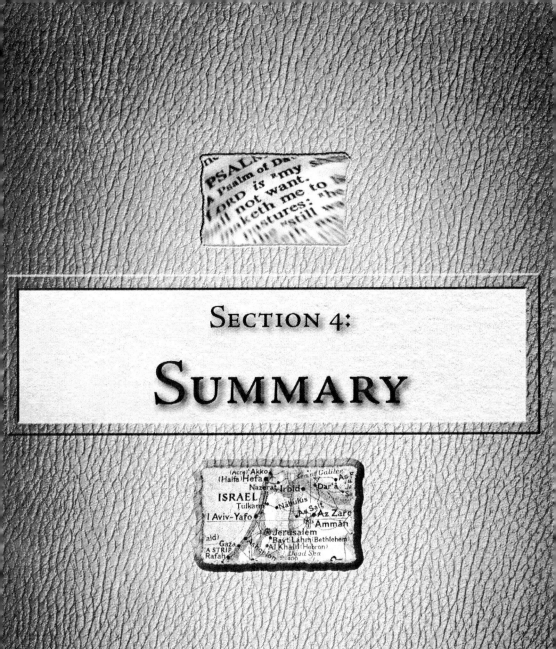

Section 4:

Summary

12

Reviewing Key Principles

∽ Looking Back ∽

Over the course of these studies, we have watched as God's people made their way on the arduous move from Persia to Jerusalem, and we have considered the sacrifices they made to rebuild the walls and the temple. Indeed, many Jews had grown comfortable and prosperous in Persia and chose not to make the move back to Judah, simply because the cost was too high. But there were others, like Ezra, Nehemiah, Haggai, and Zechariah, who did not hesitate to pay whatever cost was required to obey God's commands.

And hardship there was. God's people faced strong opposition from very powerful enemies, enduring mockery, sabotage, false friendship, and even death threats. Beyond that, the godly leaders came to realize that apart from the new covenant and the Messiah, the people would never be able to obey the Lord as commanded. Yet through it all, God's character shines out. We are reminded at every turn that He is completely sovereign over all affairs of mankind, and we see again and again that He is faithful and true to His Word.

Here are a few of the major principles we have found. There are many more that we don't have room to reiterate, so take some time to review the earlier studies—or better still, to meditate on the passages in Scripture that we have covered.

∽ Some Key Principles ∽

This world is not our home.

The people of Judah had been carried away to captivity, but they were not made slaves as they had been many centuries earlier in Egypt. Rather, they were allowed to establish relatively normal lives within the new land, and many Jews had risen to levels of power and prosperity. Daniel, for example, had served at least three different kings as a close personal counselor. Yet this relative freedom brought a danger that the Israelites had not faced when they were slaves: the danger of complacency. Many of God's people had become quite comfortable in the Persian captivity, probably fitting in to their new society and doing well.

The problem was that God did not intend for them to make their home in Persia; their home was in Jerusalem, and He did not want them to put down roots elsewhere. God's temple was in ruins and Judah's walls lay in rubble, and the Lord grieved over that situation. He wanted His people to share those priorities and to long to return to their proper land to worship and serve God as He had ordained for them. The world in which they'd grown content was *not* their home.

This is equally true for Christians today. This world is not our home! It is not wrong to pursue a career or to establish a home, but the Lord does not want His people to lose their eternal focus. He wants them to remember that the things of eternity are what matter most, not the things of this world. Paul wrote, "Set your mind on things above, not on things on the earth. For you died, and your life is hidden with Christ in God" (Colossians 3:2–3). He was reminding us that, by being born again into the salvation of Christ, we have died to the things of this world. And if we are dead to this world, then there is no purpose in trying to make our home here. Our life is with Christ in eternity, and that is where our focus needs to remain.

God commands us to resist discouragement.

The enemies of God's people attempted to interrupt their works of obedience by causing them to become discouraged. The King James Version renders Esther 4:4, "The people of the land weakened the hands of the people of Judah," and this captures the essence of discouragement: to become weak, to sink down, to lose the ability to carry on, and to let God's projects drop from despair.

Fear is at the root of discouragement. You are faced with a circumstance that is beyond your control, and suddenly you begin to fear that it's beyond God's control as well. And if it's beyond God's control, you might as well give up now—which is, of course, precisely what Satan is hoping for. But God commands us not to give in to fear, but to strengthen our hands when they become weak (Hebrews 12:12; cf. Isaiah 41:10). The best way to do this, wrote the author of Hebrews, is to "consider Him who endured such hostility from sinners against Himself, lest you become weary and discouraged in your souls" (12:3). Remember that Jesus Himself faced immense opposition—more severe than any we will ever face—and He overcame all through the faithfulness of God and through utter confidence in and reliance upon His sovereignty.

Service is crucial, especially when it's costly.

Nehemiah lived in Persia, the greatest and wealthiest nation of its day. Furthermore, he lived in Susa, the nation's capital and one of the richest and most comfortable of the Persian cities. To top this off, he was the cupbearer to the king himself, a position of high trust and influence. He was undoubtedly a rich and influential man, high in the ranks of the most powerful nation on earth. Meanwhile, Jerusalem was very far away—a journey of two full months, and very easy to forget about.

Yet, when Nehemiah heard about the plight of his fellow Jews in far-off Judah, he mourned, wept, fasted, and prayed. What's more, he determined in his heart to forsake all the blessings and comforts of Persia, exchanging them willingly for hard work, rough living conditions, and constant hatred and opposition from God's enemies. In fact, Nehemiah was so determined to help with the work in Jerusalem that he risked his own life to get there, putting himself in peril of the king's wrath as well as making the dangerous and uncomfortable trip to Judah.

Nehemiah was not wrong or sinful when he enjoyed the comforts of Persia and the king's court; the Lord had placed him in that position, and he was faithfully serving Him. But the Lord had placed him there specifically so that he might be positioned to help the Jews at this moment of crisis, just as He had placed Esther where she could save the Jews from annihilation a generation earlier (Esther 4:14). The Lord was calling upon Nehemiah to voluntarily forsake all these blessings in order to participate in an important project, but the blessings that came from his obedience far surpassed all the comforts of the king's palace. If the Lord calls you in a similar way to forsake your comfort for the sake of His work, heed the call! You will bring glory to His name, and great blessings to yourself.

We must be alert and prepared for battle.

Nehemiah learned of a plot to slaughter the Jews who were working to rebuild the city walls, and he didn't take that threat lightly. He knew, of course, that the true protection of God's people lay solely in God's hands, but he also understood that he had a responsibility for the safety and welfare of those under his authority. Consequently, Nehemiah took strong steps to prepare for the threat of battle. What's more, he also expected all those working on the Lord's project to remain alert and well armed. It must have been a real hindrance to the work of building, which was strenuous enough without having only one hand available, but Nehemiah felt that the work of self-defense was as important as the work of rebuilding the wall. Trust in God does not lead to inaction. Those who put their trust in the care of God also put their effort into working for His glory.

Most of us do not face the threat of physical violence for our faith (although there are many Christians in other parts of the world today who do), but this principle applies at least as much on the spiritual level. Even if our neighbors are not threatening to attack us, we all face an enemy who is even deadlier than those who opposed the

Jews in Jerusalem. The devil is constantly prowling to and fro, like a fierce lion seeking someone to devour. God's people are commanded to be constantly on guard against the forces of wickedness, and we are also commanded to go everywhere well armed. Paul instructed us to carry with us "the sword of the Spirit, which is the word of God" (Ephesians 6:17). The writer of Hebrews gave further detail: "For the word of God is living and powerful, and sharper than any two-edged sword, piercing even to the division of soul and spirit, and of joints and marrow, and is a discerner of the thoughts and intents of the heart" (4:12).

A well-armed and vigilant Christian spends time reading and meditating daily on the Word of God. And like a well-trained soldier, a Christian also stays in close contact with his Commanding Officer through prayer and obedience. The military analogy, in fact, is very apt in life, because we live in a battle zone, where the enemy is constantly trying to destroy us. Therefore, as a believer, you must always "be sober, be vigilant; because your adversary the devil walks about like a roaring lion, seeking whom he may devour. Resist him, steadfast in the faith, knowing that the same sufferings are experienced by your brotherhood in the world" (1 Peter 5:8–9).

There are no shortcuts in obedience to God's Word.

Ezra had made many preparations for the move to Jerusalem. He had gathered a large body of Jews to join him, and each of those families had made all the necessary preparations involved in making a major, life-changing move. The king had also given Ezra his full blessing on the trip, providing him with a letter of authority to reestablish a Jewish community and rebuild the Lord's temple. He had also handed Ezra a huge sum of money and treasure, and Ezra probably felt a sense of urgency to get that money where it belonged. A host of people and plans were ready to go, only waiting for their leader to start the trip. And then Ezra discovered that there were no members of the tribe of Levi with him.

Now, human wisdom would suggest a "work-around" measure at this point. So many people were standing around, waiting to get started, and the king's money was sitting there waiting for theft—surely prudence would dictate an "ad hoc" alternate plan. But Ezra refused to begin rebuilding the temple without the leadership and assistance of God's selected priests, and he made this decision because God's Word commanded it. Ezra may have been caught by surprise, but he knew that the Lord wasn't. God wanted him to follow His prescribed methods, and He would take care of the timetable.

There are no shortcuts to obeying God's Word, and the Lord does not call His people to find "work-arounds" and "emergency interim methods." His Word gives clear guidance in our daily lives, the correct approach to worship and church structure, roles of authority and submission, and much more—much of which goes contrary to what the world believes today. When it comes to clear teachings in Scripture, there is no substitute for obedience.

God may use obstacles and setbacks to get your attention.

The Jews living in Jerusalem had returned to God's chosen city in order to obey His commands, reestablishing His prescribed worship practices and rebuilding the temple and walls. Yet as time went along, they found themselves suffering hardship. They were faced with drought and famine, nothing seemed to prosper, and everything they undertook was met with frustration and failure. Surely this couldn't be God's will for His people who were doing His work!

And that, of course, was exactly the case. The problem was that the people were *not* doing His work; they were doing their own work and pursuing their own goals, and the Lord had sent hardship into their lives to get their attention. This is the flip side to a principle we considered in Study 5, that Christians should expect opposition when doing the Lord's work. You'll remember, however, that we added the caveat that a Christian should not ignore opposition, in case the Lord is using it to get our attention. And in this passage, we see how He sometimes does that.

This principle holds as true for us today as it did for the people in Haggai's day. When God's people refuse to share His priorities and view the world from His perspective, He will send hardship and frustration, obstacles intended to make us stop and look up. The great irony is that when the people stopped pursuing God and focused on their own needs, their own needs were not met. The more they put in their own pockets, the less they had for themselves. When Christians turn away from pursuing Christ, they get consumed by the love of the world, which can never satisfy. True satisfaction can only be found in living for Jesus, not in the riches of the world. And often, if a Christian finds himself pursuing money rather than the Messiah, the Lord will send an obstacle or a trial as a wake-up call. When that happens, we would do well to consider our ways and renew our godly perspective, for the Lord might be chastening us in order to keep us from conforming to the world.

The Lord yearns for your fellowship.

The Lord told His people, "I am zealous for Zion with great zeal; with great fervor I am zealous for her" (Zechariah 8:2). Many modern Bibles translate "fervor" as "wrath," which captures the burning passion the Lord was expressing. "I burn for you with a jealous fire," the Lord was effectively saying, "a zealous and jealous love that will tolerate no competition." The Lord yearned so deeply for the love and fellowship of His chosen people that it was like a consuming fire, destroying anyone or anything that prevented their full reconciliation.

It is interesting that the Lord referred to the zeal of His love in this context. The Jews had been very zealous in maintaining a cycle of fasts over a period of seventy years during their captivity. "Should I weep in the fifth month and fast as I have done for so many years?" they asked (Zechariah 7:3), implying that they had not permitted anything to prevent them from this religious observance. But the Lord called them to search their hearts and question what they were truly fasting for. Were they mourning the loss of God's close fellowship, which they had once enjoyed as His chosen nation, or were they mourning over their own suffering and misfortune? The two are not the same!

The Lord wanted His people to be zealous in seeking His face and entering His holy presence. Now, this might well be associated with certain spiritual activities, such as commemorating the Lord's Supper, as Jesus commanded (Luke 22), but those activities themselves are hollow and meaningless if one's heart is not fully committed to living in fellowship with God. The Lord has a burning zeal for your fellowship, for your company, and He wants you to share that same zeal for Him.

⌁ Digging Deeper ⌁

1. *What are some of the more important things you have learned from the books of Ezra and Nehemiah? from Haggai and Zechariah?*

2. *Which of the concepts or principles have you found most encouraging? Which have been most challenging?*

3. *What aspects of "walking with God" are you already doing in your life? Which areas need strengthening?*

4. Which of the characters we've studied have you felt the most drawn to? How might you emulate that person in your own life?

↜ TAKING IT PERSONALLY ↝

5. Have you taken a definite stand for Jesus Christ? Have you received His gift of salvation? If not, why not?

6. In what areas of your personal life have you been most convicted during this study? What exact things will you do to address these convictions? Be specific.

7. What have you learned about the character of God during this study? How has this insight affected your worship or prayer life?

8. List below the specific things you want to see God do in your life in the coming month. List also the things you intend to change in your own life in that time. Return to this list in one month and hold yourself accountable to fulfill these things.

If this is the first of these studies that you have completed, read the previous titles in this series. They will greatly enhance your knowledge of the Old Testament—not to mention your walk with God.